Collecte
Volume 3, Prose
Fiction.

Nigel Pearce

chipmunkapublishing
the mental health publisher

Published by
Chipmunkapublishing
United Kingdom

http://www.chipmunkapublishing.com

'Many of the most sincere and gifted artists and writers in this capitalist world are conscious of a loss of reality.'
- Ernst Fischer: 'The Necessity of Art'.

'Literature is the lie through which we tell the truth. '
-Albert Camus.

'What is required for writing is habit.'
- Virginia Woolf.

Nigel Pearce

On literature and the search for meaning

'I was in the municipal park just now...words had disappeared and with them the meaning of things, the methods of using them, the feeble landmarks which men have traced on the surface and then I had this realization...I too was superfluous.'
- John-Paul Sartre (1965).

Nausea was a novel written by Sartre in 1934, but not published until 1938. It is in the form of diary entries by Antoine Roquentin, a solitary outsider, who decides to write a biography. However, the novel traces his transformation. The scene from which the quote above is taken is the central part of the novel and, here, asks not only questions about the nature of Roquentin's existence, but also significantly about language. Sartre would later find the resolution to these questions in a commitment to the oppressed. For as he wrote:

'It is necessary to look at man and society...with the eyes of the least favoured. The masses introduce, like a splinter into flesh, the radical demand for the human in an inhuman society.'
- John-Paul Sartre (1968).

Sartre and Simone de Beauvoir, whose analysis: 'The Second Sex' became the corner-stone for 'second-wave' feminism, are probably the best known of a group of philosophers and writers who are loosely termed 'Existentialists'. However its origins are located in the radical Christianity of Soren Kierkegaard and the vehement atheism of Friedrich Nietzsche. Or it is possible to perceive a development from English and German Romanticism.

As Samuel Taylor Coleridge, the English Romantic poet and thinker posed the question: 'Hast thou ever raised thy mind to the condition of existence, in and by itself, as a mere act of existing?' - Coleridge. (1809/1810).

A significant theme within existentialism is that of the relationship between philosophy and committed literature. As Flynn notes in his study: 'Kierkegaard's 'truth' as subjectivity is the forerunner humanism without the human, without the creative capacity which allows humans to think beyond constructing the termite mound: 'Alas, there are many things between heaven and earth of which only the poets have dreamed. And especially above the heavens: for all gods are poets' parables, poets' prevarications. Ah, how weary I am of poets!' ibid. It is not atheism that becomes the problem, but the rejection of what Sartre would suggest is the 'the gift appeal' between the author and his or her audience, it is the loss of the truly human. Sartre says, 'Though literature is one thing and morality another at the heart of the aesthetic imperative we discern a moral imperative.'
- Sartre. (1993).
By this he means what he calls the 'generosity' between writer and reader to what Sartre will call 'commitment' (I' engagement'). - Flynn (2006). What they are both addressing is the claim for an 'objective' knowledge, of God in the case of Kierkegaard, or of the 'human condition' for Sartre. Therefore, we can see a commitment to the 'emotional' and the 'lived experience' in opposition to the growth of Positivist science, the belief that 'knowledge' can be observed and measured in the

same way as a bag of flour, that had developed in the middle of the 19th century. The latter has sometimes been wrongly associated with Marxian socialism or, at least, a 'reductionist' perspective which was never espoused by Marx or Engels. Therefore, we can see a higher or 'dialectical syntheses between the Christianity of Kierkegaard and the existentialist Marxism that Sartre would finally espouse. What was the rupture between these two belief systems? It is possible to argue that it came with these words written in 1883: "When Zarathustra was alone, however, he said to his heart; 'could it be possible? That God is dead!'"

- Nietzsche (1966).

What was the consequence for the interaction between literature, and in particular, poetry of the 'death of God' for Nietzsche? It was to embrace humanism without the human, without the creative capacity which allows humans to think beyond constructing the termite mound: 'Alas, there are many things between heaven and earth of which only the poets have dreamed. And especially above the heavens: for all gods are poets' parables, poets' prevarications. Ah, how weary I am of poets!' ibid. It is not atheism that becomes the problem, but the rejection of what Sartre would suggest is the 'the gift appeal' between the author and his or her audience, it is the loss of the truly human.

Sartre says:

'Though literature is one thing and morality another at the heart of the aesthetic imperative we discern a moral imperative.'

- Sartre. (1993). By this he means what he calls the 'generosity' between writer and reader.
'It is not true that one writes for oneself. There is no art except by and for others'. ibid.
He clarifies the point:
'The dialectic is nowhere more apparent than in the act of writing. To make it come into view a concrete act called reading is necessary...beyond that there are only black marks on paper'. ibid.
It is the death of the social dialectic, the interaction between writer and reader that is the problem with Nietzsche not atheism. For there is no social for him, only what he derisorily refers to as 'the herd' and the Ubermensch or the 'superman' which he envisioned as a sort of elevated 'elite' separate from the 'herd' or masses which he also referred to as 'the worms'. Nietzsche would comment after he proclaimed the 'death of God' and made the derogatory remarks about the masses and poets:
'Life is a well of delight; but when the rabble also drink, there all the fountains are poisoned.'
-
Nietzsche (2001).
In complete opposition to this Marx was absolutely clear:
'The proletariat is the instrument of social transformation.' - Marx (2000)
and of equal importance:
'Consciousness does not determine being, being determines consciousness, it is social being that determines consciousness.' ibid.
Therefore, for Marx not only is the masses the 'instrument' by which an oppressive society will be changed, but the very nature of human awareness is social. These core concepts were influential on

Sartre from the writing of 'What is Literature?' until the end of his life. Generally existentialist philosophers have employed literature as a medium to express their ideas. From Kierkegaard's use of parables, to Nietzsche's great religious allegory, *Thus Spoke Zarathustra*, which as we have seen he used to condemn religion, Camus' The Outsider is a model for 'philosophical dramatization' and the novels of Simone de Beauvoir encapsulate her philosophical insights. Martin Heidegger as both an existentialist philosopher and an aesthetician insisted that the poet: 'anticipates and more often adequately expresses what the philosopher is trying to conceptualize.' Flynn (2006). Novelists like Dostoevsky and Kafka have captured something of the general 'atmosphere' of existentialism as do playwrights like Beckett. But what makes literature a specifically appropriate model for existentialist philosophers? A significant component of the answer lays, for the 20th century writers, in the writings of Edmund Husserl on phenomenology as a method, although not all advocates of phenomenology would accept the term existentialist. The basic concept is that all consciousness is consciousness of 'other-than-consciousnesses'. Hence consciousness is inherently outward looking, it 'intends' the 'other'. This idea is known as 'the principle of intentionality'. What are the repercussions of this discovery? Most importantly for literature and therefore the question of 'committed' literature it overcomes the question of the relationship between the 'internal' mind and the 'external' world, 'intentionality' becomes a 'bridge' between these two spheres. Phenomenology renders obsolete the problem posed by Descartes (1596-1650) who had said: 'I think therefore I Am'. Hence without the 'principle of intentionality', Descartes is trapped in the cell of his own mind, unable to communicate, he is the writer who, following Sartre above, only 'makes black marks on a sheet of paper'. So, therefore, 'intentionality' is a process which places images, thoughts and symbols consciously into the world. Flynn here is useful in applying Husserl's methodology to Sartre's conception of the imagination: 'As Sartre pointed out in an early study, images are not miniatures 'in the mind' to be projected onto an external world, raising the problem of correspondence between the inner and outer more. Rather imaging consciousness is a way of 'de-realizing' the world of our perceptions that manifests itself to careful phenomenological description.' - Flynn (2006).

Hence, following the same line of argument, if we imagine an apple we had seen previously, a careful description will show how the imaging differs from our original perception of the apple. this quite honestly tells us nothing other than the descriptive process has changed, but this is the key for writers, what they write, how they describe the apple, effects the way it is perceived by the reader. But this again would have little significance for the reader unless the writer is using the apple in a committed manner e.g. Milton's use in Paradise Lost. Let us ponder Sartre understanding of a 'committed' literature:

'The unique point of view from which the author can present the world to whose concurrence he wishes to bring about.'

Sartre (1993).
Therefore, literature is 'ideological' in its nature for the existentialist thinker and writer. But which ideology is an immense issue. When we accept the basic method of Marx's 'Historical Materialism', expressed simply, that ideas or ideologies are a 'reflex' of socio-economic moments connected with social classes, that the relationship between these classes is founded on economic exploitation and their interests exist as opposites, indeed as dialectical contradictions. That they do not exist either in the ether of Hegel's 'Absolute Idea' or trapped in the mind of Descartes, but in the conflictual material relations of concrete History. Then it is possible to comprehend what Sartre meant when he said:
'In history too, existence proceeds essence.'
- Flynn (2006).

And once accepted the consequences are inevitable. As Sartre and Simone de Beauvoir argued in the founding editorial of their magazine Les Temps modernes (Modern Times) published in 1945: 'Our intention is to change the Society that surrounds us.' ibid. Simone de Beauvoir went on to describe their vision at the end of her study of women's oppression *The Second Sex* in 1949: opposites, indeed as dialectical contradictions. That they do not exist either in the ether of Hegel's 'Absolute Idea' or trapped in the mind of Descartes, but in the conflictual material relations of concrete History. Then it is possible to comprehend what Sartre meant when he said: 'In history too, existence proceeds essence.' - Flynn (2006) And once accepted the consequences are inevitable. As Sartre and Simone de Beauvoir argued in the founding editorial of their magazine Les Temps modernes (Modern Times) published in 1945: 'Our intention is to change the Society that surrounds us.' ibid. Simone de Beauvoir went on to describe their vision at the end of her study of women's oppression *The Second Sex* in 1949: It is for men and women to establish a reign of liberty in the midst of the world of the given.

Two disciples of Nietzsche (a short-story from the 'counter-culture').

1969 is buzzing like a swarm of bees and its lovers are dissolving into an orange mist. A stereo is spewing the music of the fashionably lost. Mick Jagger's voice is licking 'The Mid-Night Rambler' from speakers which are pulsating. The dust seems to leap off them in synchronized beats with the bass line, it jumps into this room. Jeremiah, his body emaciated by the sea of speed which had frothed through his veins that are now hardened and ulcerated by the pricks of needles, smiles. He had spent many nights dancing on the periphery of nebulae and diving into the solar circle of sacrificial rite. Jagger sings: 'I'm talking 'bout the mid-night rambler, 'bout the mid-night gambler.'

Jeremiah whispers from eyes ablaze with love and then remembers to connect with his vocal cords, then with the muscles around his mouth: 'Hey Icarus, dig that chick, man we're talking Electra here, she just shot that ½ gram.'
Icarus ponders as the membrane within his consciousness twangs with the image of her body; it is gradually etched into his mind:
'She seemed fairly cool to me man.'
Icarus wraps his long arms around his knees which seem to protrude from their sockets, rolls his mind into a ball and places it in a dusty corner of the room. Here his dream machine, the plastic syringe, lies mourning the last fix. His body suddenly jerks alert:
'Jeremiah, do you mind if I change the sounds? Perhaps the Bartok, those String Quartets, just want to tune into some lunar stuff like Blake, dig.'

From somewhere deep within the recesses of his mind, Jeremiah replies:

'Cool man, I'm easy.'

Rigid structures had formed in Icarus' mind; they were clearly defined by lines of white light contrasted against a black background. Now struck with wonder he remembers reading that Allen Ginsberg had a vision of Blake. Ponders if he will have a similar experience, it brands his mind. The chains are being loosened… A lightbulb hangs by a frayed cord from the ceiling which stares back with a yellowish pallor. It seems naked, vulnerable, emitting light, but this glow is from the grid's energy. Icarus turns to his companion and says:

'Man, the white-coated one's shot that stuff through the brains of revolutionaries.' Jeremiah replies 'What stuff?'

Icarus hums:

'Electricity, they wire you up to the grid and zap, there goes the class consciousness.'

Jeremiah sighs:

'Heavy man, really heavy. Be cool just bring the whole stinking system to its knees and start again.'

'What I'm saying is, like, they the oppressors burn the brains of the innocents.'

'You seen the 'works' man, we're beginning to come down.'

'No way man, we're really buzzing now, connecting about some important stuff. I noticed you've scribbled more notes on Nietzsche in the book of the dead, that writing pad you keep stashed away.'

Jeremiah begins to crumple, but then regains his mental balance and his body relaxes into a stream of energy:

'Yea man, the book of the dead, that's the book of the living, true immolation, cool disintegration whilst embracing our separation from what Nietzsche called 'the herd', I mean the 'straights', dig, they're the blind.'

Icarus continues: 'Us, those who speed through time and space, man, we're a new evolutionary stage, apple blossom flowering on their dead wood, man we're wired tonight, last night, tomorrow, it just emerges into one Hegelian...' '... 'Absolute Idea', right, that's incarnate in us baby, need a fix?'

A swarm of bee's swirls again like the dust whipped up by a desert storm, this torment which can only assuaged by the prick of a needle, but the sting remains in an arm, in our minds. The woman, who'd mainlined a ½ gram of amphetamine, had left behind a token of her love, a small square of tin foil. She'd smiled, tossed back her head and said:

'When it's cool, do this gear and remember me.'

Her beatitude of night is beginning to caress into curves the oblong structure of this haunted room. She will never be threatened by the banality of day as the integrity of oblivion will never be threatened by the rising of sun. She is the high priestess who will celebrate the beatification of night; it is her Last Supper which Jeremiah and Icarus will share. Her name is ancient; she is Isis and has returned at these End Times to save her children from the Patriarch and his wrath which could never be quenched. She lives in the 'counter-culture'.

Jeremiah muses: 'That God stuff man, it's all finished, Nietzsche said: 'God is dead', dig.'
Icarus agrees: 'Yea, I dig, like the shrinks say you can't believe in God if there wasn't a cool bond with your father.' 'Yea, so right man.' Icarus ponders: 'Those 'straights' are weird, really crazy.'

A haze begins to encircle them, the desire to transcend this world and embrace an essence, something the 'elders' did not possess, ignites within them again. They're two outcasts of the system, but within them burnt a love of the 'Idea'. Both choose to live in the 'counter-culture' which is the body of Isis when she is pregnant with the 'Word'. A prophet of this tribe named Timothy Leary had said 'L.S.D. creates an ontological awaking.', but he hadn't intended that it should be taken intravenously!! Electra cruised back later; the sacrament had lain silently in a sea of shadows, solitary in its wrapping of tin foil, awaiting an awakening, it's benediction. She is, also, the goddess Isis and welcomes Jeremiah and Icarus to her mass, it is here she will celebrate   the 'Word', the creative energy of the universe which comes from the lunar muse, the feminine. She gently unwraps the square of tin foil with long pale fingers and holds the four green micro- dots in her hands, raises them above her forehead and says:
'This is my body, take it and eat, you will be sustained by its vibrations and given a glimpse of infinity.'
Jeremiah and Icarus genuflect before her Host and Isis places two tabs of acid on each of their palms, they then prostrate their bodies before her alter. She smiles and whispers:

'Have a good trip, never forget me.' They were dizzy with anticipation when Isis left and quickly found their dream machine, prepared the L.S.D. for a fix and located the mainline… Wwwwhhhhhhhmmmmmm without any fear of flying this room is left dancing.

A spectre of William Blake appears in its corner reciting: 'Hear the voice of the bard! Who Present, Past & Future, sees; Whose ears have heard The Holy Word That walk'd among the ancient trees.' Tangerine lights are merging into purple clocks which climb the walls, the beatification of night; it is her Last Supper which Jeremiah and Icarus will share. Voices jump from the, from the stereo Jimi Hendrix's lyrics caress: 'Purple haze is in my mind, nothing don't seem the same, excuse me while I kiss the sky.' Eight hours later the ambulance men found Jeremiah's body rigid, his eyes staring and the blood congealing in a syringe which hung limply from his arm. They found Icarus an hour later in a nearby park curled into a ball; he was repeating a mantra:

'"My name is Oedipus, my name is Oedipus, my name is Oedipus….'

He'd flown close to the sun often, this time his mind had melted, his friend had died, and Electra/Isis had fled, forced to go underground because the 'heat' was closing in.

The night becomes darker: being 17 and in difficulties.

This child had been expelled from a womb, aged 7, during the "summer of love". The place where he had lived was without love, a place of darkness, a matrix of oppression. In this place, the glare of intimidation was the god, and the angels lived in fear of another deluge of threats. These places, they are called families, are dark places. He does not know why. Perhaps it is just in the nature of these places? Ten years had passed in a whirl of tempest and fear. He had sought sanctuary in the company of souls who did not yell at him. His new companions did not have the strut of oppression and welcomed this outsider into the company of dreamers; in this place, he felt safe. These people were not branded with the iron of hypocrisy. They kissed him with potions, wondrous white powders which beckoned him into a world of meaning and caring. Initiating him into a world of compassion and the poetry of oblivion, they prepared his fix. The pristine white powder floats into a spoon, and a lighter ignites, a wait until the liquid begins to bubble with significance; cotton wool is placed, with the zeal of the mystic, into the magic liquid, and the plastic syringe sighs as the plunger is drawn up, hell will cease now, heaven's dance begins again caressing the verse in the mind of the poet. Those shackles will float away again, the needle fits snugly onto the syringe, the singer of dreams smacks his arm, the tube becomes swollen, and the spike pierces the purple vein, deliverance from the world. As the plunger draws upwards, a serpent of blood dances into the cloudy liquid. Thank god, a hit the first time, the plunger pushes this chemical dream out of the syringe into his arm, he trembles ahrrrrr…he warmth radiates up the arm rushing into the catacombs which were his mind….this heat begins to permeate the entirety of his body, he is blessed into the Kingdom, the stigmata on his arm are aching with knowledge now: peace dawns with lilies floating in a pool of violet…this is the innocence denied him as a child.

A crisp autumn wind caresses brown and blood-red leaves into a frenzy of swirls. The psychiatric hospital sits alone in the platitudes of the rustic. It is where light is reciprocated between the damned, on occasion. The outsiders, ostracised by a world of squares which cannot accept circles, seek sanctuary in this place of shadows, a place of vibrations. The ambulance cruises through a bleak but welcoming afternoon; he hopes the hospital will be like a monastery, a convent where the tragedy will be saturated with love. What strikes him when the nurses help him undress is the crisp institutional nature of this place. The bed has white sheets. They feel like there have been bleached. The nurses wear the uniform. The women are dressed as nurses in a general hospital, the men in identical hospital suits. A doctor in a white coat drift onto the ward; he smiles:

'Nurse will give you an injection. You are safe here. I'll see you soon. Rest the mind and build up your body.'

'Thank-you. I'm quite interested in Jung's work.'

'We will talk about many things, but rest now.'

Two nurses puzzle the poet, lost in a dance of the tragedy and ego which pervades these places. They carry a grey cardboard tray. Its edges are raised to prevent any deviance from the task allotted by the god in a white coat. On it is a plastic syringe, the same model used by the dreamers, around this howling labyrinth of unquiet spirits, and the exorcism begins. Words drip like droplets of sweat from their tight mouths:
 'Now we can do this the easy way, or you can make it difficult.'
The dreamer is metamorphosed into a patient, he lies resistant, but he recognises in their eyes something of the priest draped in black, preparing to utter words of absolution. The needle is eased into hard muscle; it is painful, a Largactil daze strikes his body like the thud of thunder in a prison cell, and the mind does not begin to relax; there is nothing vaguely opiate about this chemical. Instead, it is like being struck by a truncheon, battered by the blows of mediocrity.
        At the foot of his bed sit two nurses, his sight focuses on them, but he becomes aware of other beds, two lines of iron bed frames on which are mattresses with alternate orange and lime green covers. On these ships of dreams, within the house of whispers, sit these mystics of the psyche. Ten days on, and he can wander around the ward, the watchful gaze of the uniformed ones observing his tracks of body and mind. The voice of the ward's patriarch booms through the ward:
Medication time, come and get your pills, everyone.'
Those shackles are about to be locked again as an orderly queue forms. Does the poet ponder that

this may be a form of victimhood? But who are the victims: patients or nurses? The rigid frame of the clinic's entrance anticipates the medication. It is blocked by a steel trolley, behind which stand two nurses. On its top lie ordered rows of medicine tots awaiting the sticky brown syrup: chlorpromazine. The taste is foul and the odour unpleasant. It slips down the throat like swallowing the Sulphur of Hades. However, this young man empathises with the flowers of the night, and he becomes aware that he has found his home, the asylum. Gradually the poet learns the rules and mores of this place. He grasps the nature of the hierarchies, the manoeuvring of staff and patients, and the look of fear which registers in the eyes of some when approached by a certain nurse. The life of this organism resounds in his mind. He can resist actively or passively, on occasion, to defy the authority of this place, other times to play the role of submission, to appear broken; it's all part of living in these places, it's the way you learn to survive. But his mind is never subordinated before their high alters of absurdity with those candles which burn like acid in the soul. Of course, there are caring staff; he learns to seek them out, other outsiders who also seek sanctuary in the hospital, but on the other side of the fence, sometimes the boundaries become rather confused when we live in this place. Some of the nurses sing a similar song. It is 1977, and the world still inhales the breath of revolution; we are dizzy with vision, each other and ourselves. However, the revolution has its enemies in these places.

As evening caresses this tormented place, the poet decides that the revolution should be alive in

21

this palace of dreams. He resists with his body; his body is like a weapon which cannot be soothed with the language of oppression. This resistance is the poetry of darkness; it is the drama of the physical, so he begins to refuse food. A week later and he becomes accustomed to the ache of hunger in his stomach and the verse which is his defiance. The retreat into the damp cell of the body becomes a reason for existence, and his sigh to the night has become a song with all the oppressed. The situation begins to tighten like an elastic band which is gradually stretched until its tension winds up to make a doll dance. The nurses are not detached from the drama, they are part of this scene, and the atmosphere begins to become heightened as his refusal of food enters its fourth week. The white-coated ones come to check his blood pressure on the hour, and he is transferred to the disturbed unit. Here electricity buzzes every breakfast between the poet and the nurses; they want him to eat the greasy bacon and beans shuffled before him. The struggle reaches intensity again at lunch and returns like a rat-invested plague as tea-time approaches, but his poetry still flows with the ink of memory and the frost of autumn in these places.

Venus also lives in the disturbed unit. She is 18, has shoulder-length ginger hair, crimson cheeks and a ribbon of freckles across her nose. She wears faded blue denim jeans and an orange tee shirt. Venus is huddled in a wheelchair. The poet wonders who she is, is she "cool", or perhaps she's a real human being? Venus and the poet are like flowers in a wasteland of twisted iron. They soon become aware of a reciprocal vibration:

The bastards, I jumped, wanted to fly and die, know what I mean?' she aches.

'Yes, yes, I do; I want to bring this rotten edifice crashing down with me. They're the living dead, and you know Jesus said: "Let the dead bury their dead".

"My name is Venus: I take acid and speed, do you?'

'Yea, I do.'

'Venus smiles and says: 'Let's trip in the bin'. Their conversation is the dialogue of dreams in the dream factory, the asylum, but these visions can be aborted. The staff have removed her wheelchair and hidden it somewhere on the ward. They say she can walk, but Venus's legs are smashed, and the nurses know this. They don't like young people with a vision that defies a world with its stone-grinding lives into the flour of platitudes. The nurses sit on cheaply upholstered wine-red chairs at random points around a white-washed room. They stare with eyes which burrow into your most hidden being, and there is no escape here. One method of control is to take the patient's cigarettes and issue them hourly; the hours begin to revolve around the next cigarette, this becomes the accepted form of communication in these places, and all other forms of human contact have been frowned upon in the unit. In this place, when you're 17 or 18, resistance becomes the ideology of despair, and this gradually becomes the only hope, the dream.

It is Sunday, and as usual, the porters bring the meal trolley. It is a steel box with draws which contains dinner, then beneath pudding; on each corner is a castor with a black rudder tyre. The nurses plug it into a socket, and the tension rises. Venus needs a cigarette, she must drag herself across the floor to the charge nurse's office, and she understands the process of subordination on this ward:

'Please, nurse, may I have a cigarette.'

A snapped reply: 'You know there aren't any.'

We all know Venus's mum brought in 20 at visiting time the evening before:

'Please nurse, a smoke.'

'Clear off.' Is the response.

'I only want a smoke.'

'If you carry on, there's an injection. You don't want that, do you?'

Venus pulls her broken body across the carpet; tears wash the pain from her face, and she sobs silently.

These places could be like the everlasting night. The poet sits at a white vinyl-covered dining table. He feels dizzy. A nurse pushes a plate of cabbage, sprouts, roast potatoes, beef and gravy before his trembling face:

'You will eat today. You will eat this.'

His silence has more resonance than any shout. The ward-sister slams a food liquidiser on the table, it has a brown square base, about 4x4 inches, on top of this is a cone shaped container, his dinner is slopped into this, the lid is snapped into place, a button pushed, there is a whirling noise, the product is a thick green liquid, the cap is removed. The contents poured into a beaker:

'You will drink this, now!'

'I'm not drinking that slime.'

Lightning between patient and nurse sizzles and sparks. They surround him. One gives him a poke

in the ribs, and their loud voices sting his mind; this seems, to him, like a manifestation of Dante's worst dreams. The torment continues. Eventually, he agrees to drink their potion and swallows the green slime. His stomach contracts and expels the liquid; he spews uncontrollably. Before the poet lies a pool of yellow vomit and green bile. They demand: '
Clean that up immediately.'
This sounds, to the poet, like an expulsion of the Fallen from heaven; he is cast into an abyss of fear where the flames of their anger lick his soul and body in the frenzy of domination:
'I'm not cleaning that up; you made me drink the stuff.'
He was 17, and the night had become very dark. It will be over a year before he will see the outside of the hospital, and the doctors never did discuss Jung with him. The only comfort for this poet was to scribe the voices of other outsiders in his verse.

.   .

The Goldfish Bowl and Beyond.

An experience of the Fire, Rescue and Prevention Service.

The poet was in a heightened state caused by intravenous diazepam. It had been given to sedate him during the heart procedure to implant a double chamber pacemaker and remove a loop heart monitor. The latter had recorded that his heart had stopped for twelve seconds…twelve seconds. He had ruminated upon this. Dr Krishna had said he was lucky to be alive and, indeed, because of the oxygen starvation to the brain to have no cognitive problems.

He was trying to explain the vicissitudes in the life and writings of Alexandra Kollontai to two women. Why, well, it is pretty simple as there is a framed black and white photograph of her on his flat wall. There are many writers and artists woven into the tapestry of those walls, his home. As there had been into his life. Is not the boundary between everyday life and fiction blurred for you as well? Maybe not, I do not know. Two women had rescued me, let me tell you because the ward had seemed like a giant aquarium. This was because he was used to a goldfish bowl. One had asked: 'Who is the woman in the picture frame' and thirty or so minutes later, they both had politely listened to a brief biography as well as the accompanying bibliography of Kollontai's writings, both non-fiction and fiction.

But how had this all begun? I left Waterstones with a new book of poetry and simply zonk; I was unconscious on the pavement. It happened twice again, but these were apparently 'faints.' That happens to people with mental health issues. We faint for no apparent reason, obviously. However, one morning in my goldfish bowl, I was on the phone to an academic, a Doctor of Creative Writing and, once again, was zonked and dropped the phone. When I came around and orientated myself, she was somewhat concerned. I had not been talking gibberish but discussing poetry for a Master of Arts in Creative Writing with the Open University. She told me firmly yet with a certain gentleness to phone the GPs. This time a different doctor was 'duty' and, having known me for some time, referred me to Dr Krishna. The loop heart monitor was fitted by Sister Serendipity, and we have come in a perfect circle. Or so you might have thought.

The two women who brought me home and who I had been chatting about Kollontai with were from the Fire, Rescue and Prevention Team. Moreover, these were not one-dimensional women. There are those of us who circle goldfish bowls because the river's currents were too forceful. Then people like Eileen and Tracey follow us up, befriend us and provide that essential connection to humanity. This is because no one transmogrifies into a fish or flees the river of life without a cause or often numerous counter-epiphanies. We just need a little coaxing, support, and some practical help to begin to write in the golden notebook again. It is here where people rather than scaled amphibians scribe their lives. This is an awful freedom, but it makes one human again. 'Thank you!!'

The Red Woman.

A chill gust of wind swept frosted and contorted leaves across the car park in a frenzy of copper brown and red. John held on tightly to his diary; another one discharged, and his caseload was heading for the quota set by management. A glint of satisfaction which was almost reptilian appeared in his eyes as he glanced, almost glared, upwards at the grey and black clouds. John pulled out a copy of Goethe, Faust, from his jacket's inside pocket, but hardly noticed the tatty book other than to glimpse the cover subliminally. Its contents were devoured at university on the new rapid process social work degree. His attention was settled on the meeting that he had just left:

'Yes, that is another box ticked, empowering the clients.' He said, smiling to himself.

After all, that is what it said in that shiny new social work textbook he would have read, and he appears to be the incarnation of modern social work. That smile was so different from his clients. It exposed a perfect set of glinting teeth. Of course, John cleaned his teeth twice a day and went to the dentist every six months, unlike his clients who neglected their appearance.
Was he a man on his way up to heaven, maybe? The social worker closed his car door; it looked secure, just like an iron womb. The 'in' ambient music of Brian Enno caressed him in full surround sound; he looked safe and significant in his world, His diary:

October 2nd, 2009:

Pam: 10.00-10.30, [Goal, there is not anyone known to us in bed with her]. Lunch with Luscious Lesley, the new secretary.

Stephen: 1.30-2.00 [Post-discharge visit, isolated, no family, potential suicide, but intellectually competent]. Note to self, and this was quite a coup. He has
been on the books for years.

And so, it continued.

A middle-aged woman watched him; she had remained obscured. Her name was Angelina, and she kept copious notebooks. She wrote on one which was battered and torn. It was a hotchpotch of memory, observations, and analysis. Angelina opened her notebook:
'Lotta continua.'

These two words must have sliced like fragments of memory into her heart as she recollected those chilly hot Brigade Rossi days which had possessed her youth for she almost tore her notepad and wrote:
Burn baby burn.

She gripped a black pen with such passion and held it so rigidly in her hand, which had almost become a clenched fist, that it spurted ink. She wondered in her book of memories:
How had Brigade Rossi lost, but of course we had not? No, it was merely a setback along the

necessary road of dialectical conflicts, which cluttered the route to existing socialism.

She paced restlessly with thoughts trapped in her head like particles in The Large Hadron Collider. Today she stands rather like a resurrected Rosa Luxemburg, described by Clara Zetklin as 'the living flame of revolution.'

Stephen, who was recently discharged by that strutting cock of a man. He did not keep a diary; he hadn't needed one but kept verse in a stash tin in a secret place and travelled light.

Like a feather that is blown higher and higher on the exhalations of the Earth's autumnal wind which became more like the icy gusts and gales of winter. He plummeted one morning, and

then he realised help was much needed. There was not any, so he went to see 'the Man'.

Angelina was whispering about with her notepad when she clocked the young man rolling one spliff more than was good for him, spaced-out is not adequate to describe his state of mind; zonked but conscious seemed to be rather a more suitable assessment she thought.

'Hey cat, where do you live, where's your pad.' She spoke with kindness. 'Hi, are you some Madonna.'

'No.' she laughed, 'No, not me.' This was the first-time laughter had rung spontaneously through her for a long time.

'I thought you were Our Lady of The Angels, come to take me higher. To hold me in your arms and escort me to heaven.' He grinned.

'Hey babe Icarus, now don't get to fly too close to heaven. It might not be what you expect. But where do you crash, the 'heat' will pull you, be careful.' 'Nowhere.'

She carefully removed her grey flannel jacket, an old companion, and wrapped it around the shoulders of the young man. She held him in her arms and by the rocking rhythm of a lullaby calmed him. There was not an alternative, he needed shelter, and she took him to her concrete nest. Inside the sparsely furnished one-bedroom flat was a disproportionately large collection of books. They were on shelves built with wooden planks resting on reddish house bricks which formed columns at each end, but the books still overflowed onto the floor. Angelina possessed no cooker, but a kettle and an old microwave to heat food. Purple drapes were hung permanently across the small windows. Unshaded electric fitments provided the interior light. She laid cushions on the floor of the area which doubled up for a kitchen and a library and lowered him onto this bed; he was almost comatose with the amount of skunk he had smoked and hashish cookies that he had gobbled. Although she knew his life was not at risk, you do not O.D. on cannabis, but you can take it too far. She removed her jacket from his body and covered his ragged clothes with a thick red covering with green and blue mermaids embroidered on them.
'Babe Icarus, you glide softly.'

He was unconscious for forty-eight hours, yet Angelina remained awake and alert for the whole

of those two days and nights. She wandered around, wiping the sweats from his body like a moth drawn to a flickering light.
On the third day he said:

'Hi, who are you? Where am I? I mean, how did I get here?' 'Stoned and incapable.' Smiled Angelina.
A hot flush of embarrassment coloured the young man's face.

'Don't worry, babe Icarus, you were too stoned to walk, let alone anything else. See that rectangular brown thing and a small oblong of lighter stuff. It is bread and cheese, help yourself. Those blue things to your right are jeans which should fit you, and the white thing next to it is a cheesecloth shirt. See you in ten.'
'Oh?'

They would converse carefully, feeling, and then plucking strings of the instrument which they were tuning in to each other's wavelengths:
'I don't know your name.' 'Either do I.' She replied.
 'That's a funny answer, do you always talk in riddles.' 'That is no riddle, babe Icarus.'
 'That's my new name, is it?' 'Maybe so.'
'Okay.'
'That's settled then; you have been named!' 'Okay, boss.' he smiled.
She grimaced and flinched:

'Never, ever call me "boss" again, you understand that. Never use that filthy word to describe me, anyone, but them and their lackeys.

'What's wrong, I was joking. Heavy stuff. Are you like one of the shrinks, which we used to see or those social workers? You know when they smile you first see perfect teeth, but the mirage wears off, then you see their fangs.'
'I am sorry. No, I am not a shrink or a social worker. Here, have you ever worn a kaftan; one would suit you.'
She popped into her bedroom and produced one like a magician (it was quite a relic she had dragged around on her wanderings). She measured it on him for size:
'Hey, you will make a hippie yet.'

And they smiled and hugged each other as if they had been lost in a labyrinth and finally found a companion to help them escape. At least to accompany one another on those interminable journeys which exist within any maze. She wrote later in her journal, recalling a quote from Albert Camus which she inscribed slowly and contemplatively, like a nun in an enclosed convent:
'Autumn is a second spring when every leaf is a flower'- Albert Camus."
However, this ballet, this Prokofiev ballet is like the Shakespearian drama from which it took its name. Why? Because Angelina and 'Babe Icarus' were two more "star crossed lovers."
She glanced with an intensity and wrote:
Does his mind resemble 'the dark night of the soul' that St. John of the Cross had written about in his poetry and anticipate ecstasy.

'Babe Icarus, tell me about those visions and voices. What the shrinks call your illness, is it Schizophrenia.'
'It isn't an illness at all, you see. I am both blessed and damned in equal measure like William Blake was and Blake lives in me. I am also the Fallen Angel from Milton, Paradise Lost and because I descended into The Inferno of Dante, so I always say: 'Abandon hope, all you who enter here.'
'Babe Icarus, I wouldn't tell you what to do, but possibly the skunk and the hashish for some people are not the best if they have certain proclivities. Marx said: 'Religion is the opium of the people, it is the sigh of the oppressed creature.'
He fell silent and then marched out of the room.

A gradual, but discernible change occurred from then onwards. Angelina and Stephen were after all of different Houses. Late-autumn became mid-winter; Angelina knew there would be no thaw as she penned in her diary:
December 15th:

'Now is the winter of our discontent.'
    – William Shakespeare."

Either forgetfully or with subconscious intent she carelessly threw it to one side on that fateful day:

'Angelina, what is this book I found on the bed.'

'Oh, I don't know, you tell me. Explain it to me, and then I shall ravish both
 your analysis and you.'

'What is Brigade Rossi?' Does it mean Red
Brigade, no not those, not those
terrorists?'

She froze as surely as if struck by a bolt of ice,
then shattered into fragments and melted into the
heat of rage, tears boiled, poured out of her eyes
with uncontrollable body jerking sobs:
'No, never, we were not terrorists. We were
fighting for freedom.'

He rushed out of the flat without dressing,
screaming as he ran through the network of
streets to the Social Services Department. It was
locked as it always was for security reasons, staff
safety. Still, there was no one at the desk and just
a note taped across the intercom:
We are sorry, there is no one available at present,
please ring and leave a message, and we will get
back to you as soon as possible.

It was the Christmas staff meal. Stephen ran to
the Roman Catholic Church, but a note had been
permanently attached to the church door. The rain
had defaced it slightly:
Mass was cancelled due to a shortage of priests.
You are always in our prayers. In an emergency,
seek appropriate help from the Social Services or
dial 999.
The young man cried out:

"666' it is written in The Book of Revelation, and I
am now marked as the Evil One.'
He became deranged and threatened to burn
down both the Social Services Department and

the Church. A passer-by made a mobile call to the police who responded and alerted the psychiatric team. The social worker arrived first and had rushed to get there because he had discharged the young man. Angelina also arrived, breathless, and confronted him; she pulled out a small Lugar pistol in a whirl of black and grey:
'Now just give me that gun. Steady, you must be ill, a very poorly woman.'

'Don't patronise me. My name is Angelina, I am a revolutionary, and you are a pig, a muttonhead. You will never put him back in that place, the so-called hospital.'

She pulled the trigger again and again and yet again, emptying the small magazine: 'Now that is another box ticked don't you think, eh.'
Then spat onto the hunched figure of that moaning man and calmly walked away like a whisper into the wind.
The web buzzed with one more suicide. Another had jumped from Beachy Head onto those rocks which are pounded by a relentless and remorseless sea. The body, what remained of it, after the sea thrashed it, was torn, bloated and blue. A note was found nearby the cliff edge hidden under a bush and weighed down with a stone and inscribed:
" My name is Legion, for we are many."
          - Mark 5:9.

Some rumoured that a mermaid could be seen; she swam around the cliffs ceaselessly, carelessly without concern and gambled her life upon those waves as they crashed onto the wailing, desirous and deadly rocks. The mermaid's name could have been Angelle or Angelina, even Angel, some of the local Cornish people, muttered amongst themselves. They believed this to be true because many had claimed to have heard her wail something like that name as she played Russian Roulette with each tide. Does anyone really care but the sea, the sea, the dead sea

Commentary.

Always in the short story there is the sense of the outlawed figure wandering on the fringes of society…
(O'Connor, F 2004, *The lonely voice: a study of the short story.* p,18).

I began in medias res; John has already discharged Stephen and Angelina is a mature woman who had fought with Brigade Rossa in Italy. Left urban guerrillas were eventually pardoned in the same way Red Army Faction and June 2nd Movement prisoners were in Germany after numerous institutional deaths. However, Angelina and John are in ideological conflict, one being an agent of the State and the other attempting to topple the state apparatus. This drew immediate attention to one axis of conflict. But John is a 'false protagonist' who acted as an 'authorial hook', only to be used as a 'framing device' that draws attention to my characterisation process. Thus, the P.O.V. I had chosen, which was 'third-person omniscient' had less 'distance' between the narrator and Angelina. An epistolary form helped drive the work and helped provide another dimension for information and emotional texture. The intertextual sources were Ernest Hemingway, For Whom the Bell Toils, Political Realism from a third-person omniscient P.O.V. Mary Shelley, Frankenstein and Alice Walker, The Color Purple, Epistolary stories. Gabriel García Márquez, One Hundred Years of Solitude, Magic Realism.

John, the social worker who falls into the category E.M. Forster would call a 'flat character' as he elaborates here in a comment on Charles Dickens:

Dickens is significant. Dickens's people are nearly all flat (Pip and David Copperfield attempt roundness, but so diffidently that they seem more like

bubbles than solids). (Forster, E M. Aspects of the Novel p. 71 Hodder & Stoughton. Kindle Edition.)

Angelina is, I would argue, a 'round character.' Forster argued in their purest form: 'they are constructed around a single idea or quality; when there is more than one factor in them, we get the beginning of the curve towards the round. (Forster, E M. Aspects of the Novel (p. 67). However, regarding 'plot' Forster disagreed with Aristotle because of advances in psychoanalysis, particularly the 'unconscious'. He continued: "Character, claimed Aristotle, 'gives us qualities, but it is in actions – what we do – that makes us happy or the reverse.' He further argued: 'We have already decided that Aristotle is wrong, and now we must face the consequences of disagreeing with him. 'All human happiness and misery' said Aristotle, 'take the form of action.' We know better. We believe that happiness and misery exist in the secret life, which each of us leads privately and to which (in his characters) the novelist has access. And by the secret life, we mean the life for which there is no external evidence, not, as is vulgarly supposed, that which is revealed by a chance word or a sigh." (Forster, E M. Aspects of the Novel (p. 83). [ibid]. Although accepting some of the gains of psychoanalysis

and indeed, psychotherapy, both Freud and
Jung's work on literature. I would argue that
Aristotle's ideas in Poetics are here correct,
namely:
[…] for tragedy is a representation, not of men, but
of action and life.
(Aristotle Poetics (Penguin, 1965 p.39).
So where does this leave the question of 'plot'.
According to Forster:
Let us define a plot. We have defined a story as a
narrative of events arranged in their time-
sequence. A plot is also a narrative of events,
the emphasis falling on causality. 'The king died,
and then the queen died' is a story. 'The king died,
and then the queen died of grief' is a plot.
The time-sequence is preserved, but the sense of
causality overshadows it. [...] Consider the death
of the queen. If it is in a story, we say: '
And then?' If it is in a plot, we ask: 'Why?
-        E.M. Forster, Aspects of the Novel (p. 86).
An element of my story that is plot driven is the
dénouement. A suicide of biblical
ramifications because the suicide note referenced
the swine throwing themselves off a precipice after
Jesus of Nazareth had committed the demons of a
possessed man into them. While someone with
the Latin root name – 'angelic', used in many
languages, is transformed, maybe by the suicide,
into a mermaid and awaits an inevitable death like
her lover as she rides the tides at Beachy Head
As Georgi Lukács, I understand no inherent or
'world-historic' gain in the genre of Socialist
Realism. Nevertheless, that genre produced some
notable work. Especially, Maxim Gorky (Mother,
Moscow, Progress Publishers, 1965) and My

Universities, (Moscow, Foreign Languages Publishing House, 1953) as well as Alexandra Kollontai, Love of Worker Bees, (London, Virago,1988.) As Lukács argued, Critical Realist literature was often better written and offered both depth and diversity. Realist literature can generally be understood as the response to Romanticism's Pantheism and reflected capitalism's development and extremes.

For Lukács Critical Realist literature would not merely mirror the reality of capitalism as in Zola's Naturalism. Instead for Lukács, it would show the fragmented and contradictory 'typical' relations of capitalism. His understanding of aesthetics was primarily derived from Antiquity, Kant and notably when young by Hegel. Before 1916 he described himself as a 'romantic anti-capitalist' understanding the latter as alienating and lacking what he regarded as the organic unity of Ancient Greece. At least in its early period, the October Revolution in Russia provided him with a solution to the 'subject-object' problem posed in Western philosophy with the proletariat's collective class consciousness. Therefore, following both Hegel and Marx, with a lesser influence of Weber, he argued the proletariat had an 'ascribed consciousness' which would find ultimate fulfilment as 'the identical-subject-object of history.' Lukács (2010 History and Class Consciousness Pontypool, p. 258-259). However, the reader could indeed ask if Angelina aspires to Lukács' Realism or not. She is undeniably a character who exposes the contradictions of capitalism.

Nevertheless, I had foreshadowed Angelina's metamorphosis into a mermaid with the mermaid embroidered quilt with which she covered Stephen. She also 'shows' a spectrum of emotions through her actions, dialogue, and diary entries. In the same sense that Juliet was the female protagonist, and Romeo the male protagonist. In The Red Woman, both Angelina and Stephen are confronted by society's antagonists, bureaucracy, their pasts, and Fate. A 'ticked' box is the motif utilised to frame the Realist story as John's beginning and end.

Idiomatic dialogue is another device that drives the plot. I have employed poetic devices, e.g., anthropomorphism, alliteration, assonance, rhythm, to enhance my prose. I have also learnt much about the story, plot, and idiolectic usage, potentially enriching my poetry.

Janet, you were on my mind.

"if you can't adapt yourself to living in a mental hospital how do you expect to be able to live 'out in the world'?" How indeed?"
- Janet Frame (2012) p.34.
The mists were leaden with the hum of significance, a salience of silence. A cave, a fire and some shadows lingered beyond the cave. However, as in Plato's allegory only the 'philosophy- peers' were privileged to see the shadows, the 'Forms'. I had an intense interest in ab- tractions. Nevertheless, I pulled the heavy burgundy velvet curtains of my study closed. it was a foggy, chilly twilight and the screams of my patients were reverberating in my head. The year was 1957, the country New Zealand and the hospital Seacliff Lunatic Asylum. I treated one young woman patient who had been a student teacher, an undisclosed, at the time, aspirin overdose. She had continued to university where she wrote a story about her depressive breakdown. her English lecturer who she was infatuated with, or so the notes say, showed it to one of my superiors at this asylum and so would begin an odyssey. Janet Frame had been detained in in 1952; I was to meet her nearly five benumbed years later.
I had a call from Auckland six months before I met Janet, followed by a paper chase of cor- respondence, but I reached the end. I was awarded funding to head a program into Rehabilitate- and Creativity. For me it was like Manna had started falling from Heaven. However, all that seemed possible in the short term were

incremental changes to the system and some basic activities. Weaving and assembling stools, free expression art classes and the begin- nings of a group of handpicked patients who would use Freudian 'free association' to create a group poem or story. The patients in this group would be pre-surgery. I was given free rein and of course an ex-undergraduate, however disturbed the patient, and seemed an ideal candidate. and so, I met 'an angel at my table', Janet Frame, apparently a fledgling author. I sought out Miss Frame. She was huddled in the corner of a padded isolation cell, a padded cell. She looked like a bird that had flown into a plane of glass blinded by a snowstorm, in- jured, bewildered and frightened. She seemed a broken person: teeth pulled out, ill-fitting dentures, ulcers around her mouth, but had with an uncontrollable mop of red hair. I was now a little further up their Tower of Babel, a senior registrar. This provided me with a certain degree of autonomy. Although I couldn't challenge the demigods, the consultants, I could not make decisions independently of them.

'Miss Frame, um, may I address you. Janet,' I said tentatively.

'I don't want it., I don't love paraldehyde, they said Shelia did and then she died.' 'Janet, I am so sorry about your friend.'

'She wasn't my friend, but they killed her. It was wrong.'

I felt like the collective hand of the patients was going to slap me. What could I say.? An uneasy silence filled the vacuum between us, but at least that was a beginning, I thought. Better than the descent into the inferno. You can fill a vacuum, with something, respect, compassion, even friendship.

'They call me an educated bitch.'

'That is unfortunate, Janet, but not all the patients are as well read, as educated as you. You mustn't take offence.'

'No, the nurses do.'

Unprepared my response was one of incredulity, then sympathy for this sad woman. 'Do you hear many voices, Janet, like God or Keats? Emily Dickinson, maybe? Your fellow writers?'

Fool', she screamed. 'but you are no "Holy Fool" in rags.'

'Nurse, Sister - quickly, restrain her, then the medicine, the usual dose, it will have been written up in her notes.' I reacted robotically.

I nipped into the doctor's consulting room, took a small leather lined hip flask from one pocket and had a quick gulp of the medicine, the whisky, and a peppermint popped a peppermint into my mouth almost simultaneously with the other hand. My hands were trembling.

Janet's consultant prescribed a course of E.C.T after this incident. It seemed inappropriate to me, almost punitive. No patient reacts well when their symptoms are challenged. It is like challenging someone's Weltanschauung, something the most stable person would find un- settling one way or another. This was hardly the therapeutic beginning I had hoped for; I had not anticipated it. To be honest, I was angry with the male consultant: he seemed to be trying to impinge on my program. It was a question of professional boundaries, or so I thought. Now I was doubly motivated, my engines were in gear and smoking: my project and my professional pride. I knew this was a pivotal moment in my chosen career, but I hadn't realized it would become something of an 'Epiphany, of course not of the magnitude of a James Joyce text. After all, this wasn't Dublin and so the literary academics were saying in those quasi- literary journals, Modernism if not dead, was in decline. I had a predilection for the short story.

Have you read Ward No.6? just checking you, my reader, the an author's name was on the tip of my tongue, blazes, how on earth could I forget, the master: yes, that was it: Anton Chekhov. He is the weaver of my nightmares. I am haunted by Chekhov's character Ivan Gromov. I have been since I read that damned book. Why am I to be nailed to a cross as surely as Jesus of Nazareth was crucified upon one by that spectre of Chekhov's mind, Gromov, after all I am no Dr. Ragin? I am a doctor though, but I did not intend being admitted to my own asylum. How the hell did Chekhov con- jure that up? Seacliff Lunatic Asylum has its own little cherry orchard, but it does blossom, frost had eaten it years before... A community where the walls were wobbling with weeping and wailing, not that the walls had been built in no less a sturdy fashion as than the average monastery. So robust that not many patients left; even if they did, stupefied into submission by the great machine of cogs and wheels of the institution, they would be unable to compete in the tragedy of a society with its cash-nexus and mind ant marching conformity. I can tell you that many of my patients were not clinically ill, but people whose face didn't fit the necessary identikit picture at the right time. A crash, a clap of thunder heralded a downpour. Evening deepened, and I poured the first shot of that whisky which was my anaesthesia, then a second and when I woke in bed with a hangover, there was no memory of leaving my study to the quarters attached. For, yes, we doctor also lived in the asylum, but in houses, not dormitories.

I was beginning to have to justify the funding for my project; it had begun to look overly ambitious. Yes, I had a stockroom of wooden stools with woven seats, piles of randomly bespattered paper, the artwork, but nothing which was going to get me really noticed, nothing for the CV which would clinch a consultant's post. Of all the patients there was the only one whom I knew that had a history of writing: Janet. I Page | 115 parachuted down from my deluded heights and I realized the magnitude of my task. 900Nine hundred patients, drugged to the point of stupefaction; insulin therapy had wreaked havoc; E.C.T being used as a method of control, indeed in some cases as punishment and there was a culture amongst most consultants of wait, then wait again and then apply the scalpel to make them free. Where were they when the news of the medical experimentation on patients in Nazi Germany was seeping out after the Nuremburg Trails? I couldn't get the analogy out of my mind between 'Cut makes free' and the motto above the concentration camps 'Work makes free.' Yes, they ere using the lobotomy and leucotomy on a routine basis. Women looked dazed, blank, with brightly coloured headscarves; it had a resemblance of Dante's, Inferno. I saw the words drip off the scalpel I had handed the consultant two days previously:

No room for hope, when you enter this place. Dante (2008) p.56. Janet would eventually be lobotomized; I could save her and get some decent writing, which would justify my Rehabilitation and Creativity Programme. She wouldn't be discharged, that much was obvious to me, but she would write. That would tick the necessary boxes and avoid her surgery and my career and conscience were boosted. I was saved.

'If you pumped too much gas into a balloon, it would burst. Splat!' Who said that? I shuddered, but 'The Madman' continued,

'God is dead. God remains dead. And we have killed him. How shall we comfort ourselves, the murderers of all murderers?'

Was that Nietzsche's spectre raised to haunt me? 'The Madman 'noted on his pad of dust that Janet's family had stopped visiting long ago; it was a long journey after all and the doctors always know what is for the best, the parents thought. Janet was quite happy; they had been assured, years ago. She had lost siblings in freak accidents. However, there was a younger sister who had graduated and married; she began to see dark clouds in this apparently benign forecast. She had lodged with Janet at one time, just when her older sister was apparently going insane; Janet had not seemed crazy to her. A little odd, maybe, but that was Janet. and this diagnosis, once she and her husband really applied themselves to the research, did not quite fit, and in fact into seemed wrong. Schizophrenia: it just did not make sense. The sister had known Janet wrote short- stories and, overcoming some resistance from mother and father, she rummaged, searched and sought them out. Eureka! She had found Janet's notebooks, now to read them and then show them to her husband. It could be nonsense, ravings; perhaps they were right, and she was wrong. They were only one way to discover the truth: read them, show them to old teachers, perhaps not that lecturer who had Janet 'committed' 'for a little rest' and maybe then send them away to a competition or to a publisher or something. Any clue to find out what might have happened to her sister and then act. this atrophy was unbearable. Janet's life was not a stagnant pool covered with algae, at least it hadn't been. The 'Mad Man' wrote.

I, the doctor wondered if like Dr. Ragin iwi was beginning to lose 'the plot', should there be a 'plot' as Aristotle claimed; or was I living in a different genre, the short story, which may be like the 1950's and life generally without a 'purpose', perhaps it if like Dr. Ragin iwi was beginning to lose 'the plot', should there be a 'plot' as Aristotle claimed; or was I living in a different genre, the short-story, which may be like the 1950's and life generally without a 'purpose', perhaps it is a 'seamless plot', or a tranche de vie. A doctor is not a 'free man' and must as unfree men everywhere be trapped in the 'plot' as Woolf realized that only: if he 'were a free man rather than a slave. there would be no plot.' Now back to the 'plot', against me? No, I meant Aristotle: I shall, indeed in- sist have 'a beginning, middle and an end'. The place to find the plot as every psychiatrist knows is in the notes.

Page | 116 written by other psychiatrists -, the voice of the plot, of Reason. How- ever, any writings by Janet remained only referred to, but were not actually present. What the hell? no, keep your head; have a slug of whisky.

'The Mad Man' had contrived a plot., her sister would be its agent for Janet and her sister just as Antigone and her brother shared the same 'blood', the same inheritance. Now was the time for to implement it, conjuring up a spell of purple haze which would transmute into a flying carpet carrying Janet's golden words. Janet's sister had read a notebook of her short stories and discussed them with her husband. They decided to send the collection off to a National Short story competition. it was a high-risk strategy, but there seemed little choice as it was spring 1957 and Janet had been held incommunicado for years without any visitors. It was a very hot summer, and the patients were roasting and becoming agitated. The heat was on me to deliver on this project; a lot depended on it, my career. The scalpels were being whirled in an almost frenzy now. the Head of Psychiatry had had a taste of blood and thought he had solved the enigma. A new surgical unit was being built to increase the production of the 'cure', 'lobotomize them, and leucotomize them.' was the Master Plan., that is the final solution; the best made plans can go astray, solutions can have their test tubes bro- ken and leak out to corrode the scientists, the doctors, even contaminated them. The 'madman' noted the short story collection was like a spear thrown into the heart of psychiatry. it won the first prize: Miss Janet Frame was a nationally recognized writer. The scales were not only unbalanced, they had collapsed. Our progressive doctor, - that's right, the one so concerned about his patients that he had to self-medicate with whisky - was going to be the lamb that would be sacrificed. The consultants would use that incident in the padded cell. after all the ward Sister had heard him accuse Janet of hearing voices and sanctioned the injection. It was a stitch-up. Chekhov was indeed a master of the short story and knew the human condition; well, not exactly Ward No. 6, but too damned close for the doc- tor's sanity.

He would be found years later in a cave in Thailand with an unlimited supply of opium sup- plied by whom.? He would puff on his hooker enter reveries and tell strange tales of a mental hospital, a Russian writer and a woman who became a significant writer he had once treated and cured. No-one thought these stories made sense: it was the opium and a touch of mad- ness people said. He neglected his appearance and lived in the tattered rags of a 'Holy Fool.'

'The Madman' gleefully wrote that at Seacliff Lunatic Asylum, the consultants were feverish; Janet's sister and husband were due with copies of the book for Janet to sign. Nothing for it but to put her on an open ward.

"Miss Frame, there appears to have been a mistake, an erroneous diagnosis by a senior doctor, but not a consultant, you understand. Your book has won a National competition and you are to be discharged."

'No more injections, no more E.C.T.'

'Janet, you are to be discharged into the care of your sister and her husband. We wish you every success.'

'Oh, I see,' Janet smiled dubiously.

The 'open' ward was a very different story; it had a different 'plot' and denouncement. There was no paraldehyde there, you know, of course, or maybe not, wrote 'The Madman' in his pad of dust, that they must administer it in glass syringes as it melts plastic ones. The char- acters were also different than on the 'closed' wards, deep in the dark heart of this place where there is no light. The patients here are overly stressed housewives and politely spoken shopkeepers speaking platitudes. They gave these patients, those chalky little yellow helpers, and diazepam. Fresh flowers were placed in porcelain vases every day and there was much, to Jean's relief, decent food. The nurses smiled and there were not thorns, but Colgate gleaming teeth. I can lap this up, wrote Janet in her the newly acquired book for her writing the ward sister had given her. But, the dream has been, as always, disturbed by the nasty little business: waking reality. These patients stayed a maximum of three months and the headlights of the sister's husband's car was driving through the night with the two convinced they were knights saving Jane from the darkest of nights.

'The Madman' closed his pad of dust and sprinkled it on Antigone's brother's corpse. For this story of blood and was also about inheritance, a tale of madness and sanity, of corruption and purity. It is not the biography of Janet Frame., yes, the dates were correct, and the basic facts were

correct, but it is the creation of an imagination who found an inspiration in the story of Miss Janet Frame., 'The Madman' contrived with Janet's sister and unhinged the doc- tor. Why, because every suicide of people 'The Madman' had known was etched on his heart in golden script., he had not forgotten or forgiven their tormentors until their unquiet spirits would be at rest. He pondered that Janet had flown into the cage they placed his mind into. Yes, he was also restrained and had involuntary E.C.T as a young person; he also wrote finding a path out of the psychiatric hospital through publication and academic study. The caged bird sings and sings when he or she is freed and quite often those who had locked the gilded cage did not like to hear what was said about them. However, you cannot silence a song, a story or a poem, however, particularly after it is published. It is a biographical fact that the New Zealand psychiatric authorities would not let Janet Frame 'go', even in death. One analysis of her writing claimed she had borderline personality disorder. The Madman smiles and thinks if she were alive, she would retort:
'No, I am not like you.'

A Steppenwolf sniffs the morning air.

"My mind hums hither and thither with its veil of words."
— Virginia Woolf, The Waves.

The steppes had been a wasteland of significance for the Steppenwolf and some wolf packs had revenged his mind and body when he had the misfortune to meet them: learning his nature and accepting on the savannahs and avoiding those marauding packs had been an important step after many false ones. The other place had its own deprivations that was where they the Worldings lived withal their concerns about banalities; no, the Steppenwolf preferred the meaningful desolation and had become habituated to the solitude. For didn't he have his books and writing materials. Whether he had been born here he had wondered much, if he had been born atoll seemed debatable at times after a particularly protracted and lonely trek when a younger wolf of the steppes. They had been a male wolf, from whom he often fled. and an- other called his 'mother'.
The mother had taught him the ways of the steppes, herself a Steppenwolf but one made captive and taken to a cave where she was taught to speak like a Worldling but could never quite manage their language of platitudes. But, being of a similar nature, if tamed and harnessed she taught him to listen to the winds which swept across the steppes and interpret its beauty, understand its music. The tamed Steppenwolf also taught him to record the Steppes and the World in his notebooks and fashion them into poetry and

prose and a love of sniffing that sharp morning breeze and opening a book. As I observe this surreal world I shall not deceive you with his dialogues, his life is an interior monologue which from time to time others are granted access, but his observations of you and yes you are penetrating; you cannot escape those drowsy amber eyes. This world is not the physical world of Central Asia, the Steppenwolf has two rather than four legs, yet it is not the green and pleasant land of those cursed with the fidgeting of the sane terrain, no this land is named by some mental illness, by others who be- eve, although this is by no means certain, they have a privileged knowledge of the Steppenwolf: 'Paranoid Schizophrenia.' But my acquaintance with him is one of The Omniscient Eye, not divine but one of narrator of tales, the weaver of words.

Steppenwolf was 'born to be wild' and as less the fully developed wolf was hitching down the M1, my destination Notting Hill Gate. Not yet the playground of the less than totally sophisticated children of the dollar it was then a British version of Height-Ashby. First 'lift' was off a lorry driver, quite a large articulated one, that is the lorry rather than the driver who was a pleasant man of late middle-age:

'Want a lift, how old are you?'

The Steppenwolf was dressed in kaftan, jeans and beads and with a tee-shirt. He did not re- veal the age of his body, but rather his mind.

'Come on get in, when did you last eat.' 'Like, is that meaningful man.' 'Here take my packed-lunch.'

'Thank you.' the young wolf replied for the steppes he had grown-up in where suburbia in fact the exodus to that part of London had in the preceding years been mainly one from affluent if stifling zones. Like the people of the Book of Exodus these young people believed themselves to be both blessed and consequently persecuted. all believed themselves to comprise a sort of tribe of Steppenwolfs, but some were the tribe, indeed would wan- der through magic doors endlessly with and without any assistance, no would rather tumble through them, indeed for this Steppenwolf, he would walk like a somnambulist through doors and entrances and fall over precipices. At first, he had not realized people will push you through doors and hurl one over the cliff edge. He had thought at this behaviour was confined to the land of the Worldings. How wrong can a young wolf setting out across the steppes from a world of yelling and threats, those are merely transformed into different matter, there can seem to be only dark matter at times, but he possessed the key to shut the doors both magic
and otherwise and allow the illusion of existence to be retained. The key to freedom was the written word and the word read in a relationship with the reader however anonymous that may be.
Five years later and the wolf was wandering the plateau with a haversack and the light of the moon for guidance, the pleasures of the lunar night which are enchantment and torment each in full measure, balanced precariously like a set of scales suspended from the cloud where the memory of the trial of Socrates and his death with a dose of hemlock are pervasive. He was an

outcast but did not realize it, had embraced Harry Hiller, the Steppenwolf of Hermann's novel, as a young man but of course Harry Hiller was a middle-aged man when he walked through the magic door and did not have an assortment of brightly coloured phials chained around his mind, oozing into the textures of his brain. Cast out of the wolf pack for he was a little to 'wordy' for many and not willing to act out the correct role of an albino in the specimen room for eloquent Steppenwolfs. The Steppenwolf did not pursue the tarnished calve of hedonism nor could he be a shepherd for lost sheep or a matador to slay the Minotaur. He slept on people's floors and in those old crumbling Trojan Horses, the lunatic asylums. The Steppenwolf was huddled on a park bench, the Worldings eyeing weary for its was a scorching summer's day and he was ensconced in a filthy duffle coat and a very long purple and white scarf wrapped several times around his neck, almost a sort of vestment. He was elsewhere for he was the protagonist of not one but all of Camus' novels; this was a little difficult to grasp. No certainly his mother hadn't died that morning and he hadn't experienced any kind of existential self- realization, but on that bench, day past day past day but 'The Outsider' seemed to have the clarity of a million sunrises with the dew hanging on the whispering grass. Was he Meursault, he wondered: a man of around sixty always walked his Scottish terrier through the park, past the human debris, which was the Steppenwolf, by this time the odour emitting from him must have been potent and he have looked rather unkempt?

'My name is Monsieur Meursault and am experiencing an existential crisis, are you acquainted with this.' 'Bloody hell, he's flipped.' and the dog yapped in agreement.
The police came and the ambulance and the nurses 'specialled', not allowing even to the toilet by himself. He refused to take off the duffle coat and the other patients and then the staff called him Paddington. He had a marmalade sandwich just after medication time brought by a Spanish nursing auxiliary Francis with a mug of Horlicks. The Steppenwolf wondered whether Francis was Italian and from Assisi. Then a young nurse who looked like Rupert Brooke told him quietly:
'If you want to leave, you must stop this high-fluting conversation, then the doctors will think you are better. And for god's sake stop quoting from *'Dust'* by Rupert Brooke'
'But it is more than existence, it has essence, it gives life and death.' He opens the book and read the lines he knew by heart:
'When the white flame in us is gone, and we that lost the world's delight Stiffen in darkness, left alone to crumble in our separate night.
When your swift hair is quiet in death, and through the lips corruption thrust Has stilled the labour of my breath -- When we are dust, when we are dust!
-- Not dead, not undesirous yet, still sentient, still unsatisfied,
We'll ride the air, and shine, and flit, Around the places where we died, And dance as dust before the sun, And light of foot, and unconfined, Hurry from road to road, and run.

Petra daughter of the revolution. A tale about the Socialist Patients Collective (S.P.K.).

The dark allurement of revolution and sweet aroma of introspection are intertwining like phantoms in this squat in 1975. Petra, a small round woman of 19 is sitting in the smog of contemplation. Her hair is brown, untidy and short, it sits on her head like the crown of a recently resurrected Rosa Luxemburg. A brown tee-shirt with embroidered flowers around the neck emphases her plump physic and faded tight black jeans combine to say that she is a goddess of the underground and nymph of primordial night. Smiling vaguely at a middle-aged man who looks like he comes out of some 19th century Russian novel, perhaps he keeps a chronicle of the demise of his shrink into madness, she suppresses a smile:

'Comrade...but let's just cut the shit baby, what kind of crap are you lying down'. Peter slowly strokes a long ginger beard which seems temporarily, to Petra, to be creeping across the roach littered floorboards like a startled lizard. He mumbles: 'It's like the movement needs a push to tip the balance, the proletariat are in the mood for poetry, we have to become their calligraphers, you dig'.

She sighs: 'O I dig man, I really dig, know what I mean'

The rapid rattle of a typewriter sends waves of disturbance through their awareness, it's like an automatic rifle firing into a black chasm of zero, like the relentless march of the masses into nirvana, muses Petra. In her mind there are images like water forming into vapour, into clouds which sometimes obscure the sun, now they spill their seed upon soil in a shower or in a deluge, either to fertilize seed or to wash it away in a torrent. Peter is pondering whether he should scatter a little fertilizer in this garden, the Garden of Love, where iconoclasts are welcome and encouraged to participate in its rites. But he decides, with a jolt from the intellect, that everything is subordinated to the struggle. He wonders what the dynamic of the armed struggle is, some of its shadows were illuminated and a solution had surfaced during those group therapy sessions with the professor, now imprisoned himself for activities against the State and Capital, where they had discussed the dialectics of liberation. They had discovered that for them, those especially damaged by capitalism, that their situation was more complex than for their comrades without psychiatric problems, their liberation from illness was directly linked to active participation in the emancipation of all the oppressed, it must be an attempt to grasp the full implications of the "death of God", but more than that, it was to be an active assassination of God, of the patriarch and of all his oppressive relationships and the, consequent, rebirth of the child.

He murmurs to Petra: 'The struggle, all of it, is about regaining innocence lost when we were children.'

A shadow passes across Petra's face: 'Yea man, you're talking 'bout the armed struggle, call it just cool baby, self-realization, just getting rid of all the shit they put in the head.'

Peter says: '"Have you read the poetry of Sylvia Plath?'

'Of course, 'Daddy'…that's hot poetry, it's really groovy." 'Sylvia had grasped something of the essence when she wrote that line: "Daddy I had to kill you"'. Petra becomes animated; a crimson flush was rising in her face: 'She wrote those lines, there're like furrows in my mind, yea know, "Daddy, daddy, you bastard, I'm through" that's just real man, wow, so real. I've something to tell you, I'm Lady Lazarus, yea know, like in the poem'.

Peter's gaze tightens; he looks intently at this young woman:

'You attempted suicide?'

'Yea, I guess I did'.

'Do you have a name comrade?'

'They call me Petra.'

The incessant bashing on the typewriter continues without relief, it is thumping through the wall and invading Petra and Peter's consciousness. This is the remorseless beating of History: I have a name, it is Peter. Take

my hand daughter, daughter of the revolution' A loud explosion, a blaze of orange light flashes into the room, black smoke billows and then their disembodied screams reverberate in the chaos:

'Shit, man this is heavy!!'

Hard and sharpened steel voices jab them like poisoned spear heads: 'Freeze it's the police… don't move, down, get down you scum'.

Petra and Peter are thrown against the floor, then heaved up and pinned to the wall: Peter shouts: 'Resist them.'
Petra yells: 'Defy them baby, I love you.'

A Naming of the Unnamed One.

Dawn anticipated twilight and the wisdom of night.
He rolled up a rather tatty blue sleeping-bag
knowing that today would herald his Naming, a
gaining of an essence in meaningless existence.
He would dance into those rivers of darkness
which are within the self and sink into the shadow
of the black oceans which bubble within all people.
On this journey he will embrace those he meets,
who, like him, are driven
by ideas and deep passions. This Unnamed One
will find a home within the rippling chaos of reality.
With worn green denim jeans, a pink tee-shirt with
flowers lovingly sown into whirls of love and a
multi-coloured shoulder bag this young man could
have been any hippie embarking on 'the quest'.
Long brown hair complimented by an olive skin
suggested a middle eastern nature. Tall and slim,
his bangles rattled with the sweep of a languid
gait. A thirst haunted his mouth and an indefinable
hunger drove him to a working-man's café. The
tables stood like sentinels with their squeeze
bottles of red and brown sauces standing with an
ease of habit on each table. The smell of fried
food appealed, but he assuaged the hunger with a
slender glass of milk. Here the worker bees, the
drone crew, glanced at the Unnamed One with the
suspicion of medieval peasants anticipating the
next witch-hunt. Now the wind belonged not to
those bees, but to those who dreamt beyond the
hive of History. But his destiny would unravel
amongst this stream of workers buzzing their way
to work. He believed that work had become an
opiate and was a manifestation of an

estrangement separating people from their essence. It seemed like a vortex whose dance is the allurement of a drama that had dissolved. A play in which the lines had been forgotten and the theatre burnt to the ground by those who would make a cathedral for the proletariat. The Unnamed One wept with those tears that bleed down a dreamer's face. These are like the flames which have always burnt heretics, those who are crazed and caressed by flames. Our bodies are left like a burnt offering tied to the stake of oppression. The smog around him was choking and he saw a giant black heart pulsating, pumping men and women ceaselessly through a giant body which was ravaged by the pursuit of emptiness. This beat of darkness seemed to be possessed by involuntary tremors which reminded him of a leaf blown across a frozen field that cried with the cold. Walking without purpose he eventually glided into the city's park. It was vibrating with rumors of an insurrection, but this was silenced by the wailing of discarded syringes. Those accessories to bliss and death stared into his eyes and he trembled before their spectrum which was without colours. It could only provide the constant buzz of white noise which is a distraction from the silence of the void. He thought that the fear was not of the void itself, but the act of throwing oneself over the precipice. That was the anguish, the dread that one may leap into nothingness without making a conscious decision to do so. The Unnamed One looked at the desolation in this place and wondered if this ocean of unfulfilled dreams would begin to dream again if that black pulsing heart stopped its beating, its mindless pumping, stopped the thumping of people through the arteries of a corpse. Ideas wounded his body like a scythe cutting through wheatfields which has become ripe for the harvesting. Now he began to realize that the act of flinging oneself off the cliff of reason into a sea of expectations and drowning in the delights of imagination beckoned him like a poet welcomes the opium dreams. The Unnamed One became aware, it was like a message from some kind of desert hermit who had tuned into his wavelength, that absurdity and zero can only be transcended by a journey that builds icons. It must then place them on an alter which is draped in the cloth of self, genuflect before them in the night and smash the images with the passion of an iconoclast. A feeling of release overcame his temple of broken mirrors and now vision transcended introspection. Suddenly like a jolt of E.C.T. without aesthetic, the consequences of realization dawned; this storm is to be navigated. Drowning only bought a morning without the dew and it is that dew which nourishes writing. For now the desire to record this odyssey had intoxicated this young man. In the mid-morning this Nameless One drifted with the crowd's motion. A woman with a full black face rose before him like the sun dancing. She wore flowing robes of white cotton. She was surrounded, almost engulfed, by a mass of black, white, brown and yellow faces. It was a gathering of the enlightened who believed they were the damned. The Unnamed One skimmed the fringes of this flock. The woman, who was possessed by the primal gene, was speaking animatedly. She beseeched her flock to: 'Wait no longer for the Second Coming of the Lord.' She shaped them into a chalice to be filled with the wine of her belief. They must: 'Prepare yourselves to wash your bodies with the Blood of the Lamb.' She began to sigh and moan like a summer evening breeze, her words like her breathing were gaining intensity slowly, then faster, deeper and now whipped like a typhoon which reached its peak in a rush: . 'We must cast-off the soiled carcass of the World.' Most of her flock stood in a daze, their eyes glazed with lack of understanding. They began to filter away, deaf to any song which had been sung before Eden. However, a number began to chant with that primal rhythm. They became like a willow caressed, first, by a breeze, then kissed by a tempest which howls: 'We are the Saved, we are the loved, and love is the night, come Lord Jesus awake the dead.' The priestess spoke quietly now, her voice like nectar touching gossamer:

'Have no fear, for fear is death, love one another.' The Unnamed One listened with the tenderness of pain, he could see an icon of fire and love, but he knew that it was an image which reflected an absurdity, the cosmic nothingness in which people attempt to drown themselves. The priestess stood alone; she was enfolded in the profundity of solitude. He approached her and asked: 'Do you believe that Jesus was Divine.' She replied: 'Yes, he is my Lover. Have you read the bible brother?' He sighed: 'Yes, but one or two questions remain, for me, unanswered. Firstly, New Testament eschatology is quite clear that the 'Second Coming' was imminent. Jesus and the early church believed that the New Jerusalem would be heralded in and the sufferings of the 'faithful' would reach their conclusion within a generation.' She smiled with the certainty of eternity: 'The End is close my friend.' The Nameless One whispered: 'You are denying the teaching of your own Sacred Text. It is better to tune into your primal gene and vibrate with an ancient song.'

He sensed the icon was disintegrating and with compassion his mind fell upon it like the hammer of History: 'Your scripture records Jesus saying: 'Father, Father why have you forsaken me' as he was experiencing a lingering and brutal death. Surely the Son of God could not be so alienated from his Father.' The Unnamed One saw the icon crumble and its fragments blown into infinity like the dust of the dead. He felt a deep sorrow, but knew that icons must be smashed on this quest. The sorrow of those dispossessed of their icons was like a steel spike which pieced his heart. She spat: 'Get behind me Satan.' Leaving this stratum, the Unnamed One entered the labyrinthine sub-city of electric neon. Here the death bell of work did not abuse the bodies of proletarians, for here there wasn't that ethic of labour or, for that matter, the availability of work. There was a shared feel which was distinctive; a 'bee-bop' scene for those who claimed asylum with Burroughs' ghost or the defiance of thudding bass beats and the rapping of voices of the young energized by cheap cocaine and its variants. It was in this maze of heightened inactivity that the Nameless One glimpsed a few young woman and men selling a badly printed paper with its title emblazoned in red letters: 'Struggle'. The Unnamed One approached one of the young men and spoke with tenderness:

'Comrade, how many papers have you sold today?' He replied: 'About four, but you addressed me as 'comrade', are you a Marxist?' 'My interest is in dialectical materialism?' The young man's eyes shone like a lighthouse beam cutting through a foggy night: 'Yes, of course, would you like to talk?' A fire was burning in the Unnamed One's mind, he seized the moment with the embers glowing like an awaking. Speaking as if animated by tides whose motion vibrates in the night encircling the moon he began: 'Marx and Engels described religion as the 'sigh of the oppressed', but this is a concept contradicted by their atheism. A conflict between these two opposites is resolved by a 'dialectical leap'. This will, itself, produce a 'synthesis' which is the fulfilment of our human condition. But comrade, I'm sorry, it's Hegelian dialectics which are the key to this, not Marx's critique of Hegel. Do you see? It is not the triumph of matter that is in the past. Now we need the ascendancy of the 'Idea', the rise of the imagination. Its home is in Hegel.' Tears ached grooves in his face, for a belief had become enshrouded. A dream had evaporated into clouds whose rain burnt like acid. The young man replied: 'But, the struggle of the proletariat, that's my life.' He had lost his rudder in an ocean of absurdity and would drift into a vortex, spiralling into the Void. The Unnamed One continued: 'Icons will vaporize into a rite without boundaries, humans will transcend them and love shall chant her forgotten mantra.' The young man asked: 'Who are you?' 'I am nameless.' The Nameless One slipped from the city into its surrounding countryside. The corn beckoned with an

allurement which was ancient like a memory of birth before he was curled in the womb of his mother. Finding a river, he sat on the bank; a ballet of water whispered away those icons which had haunted his mind. The sun and moon shone into the river's darkness. He became aware of their motion, a metamorphosis of Light and Dark reflected from their depths. The Nameless One got to his feet and stroked himself into the water; he is Named, a child of Alpha and Omega, which is the ebb and flow of infinity. The water gulped his limps and they moved in slow motion. It was as if they were being sucked into and then suspended in a solution of syrup: 'My God, that kid has just walked into the river. Help, quick help me, he's gone under.' 'Okay mate, let's dive down and pull …come on get in.' Two men in their forties waded into the river and braced themselves. They ripped off their jackets and dived. But this river had torrents no one other than the Named One could see. Their minds became confused, and colours rushed before their eyes. Skulls seemed to rise from the riverbed beckoning them with the seduction of death. A vortex had swallowed the bile of a soul lost in the pitch of an abyss. Others on the shore pulled them free. They lay exhausted on the grassy bank. A group of labourers labourers had gathered; some were shouting, some were silent, others asked questions:
'Who was he?'
'Why did he do it?'
'I think he came from the mental home.'
'No, he was a wanderer.'

Musing of a Majnoon.

During a lull in the Infatada a young man whose
brown face contrasts with billowing pristine white
robes strode towards a group of Israeli soldiers.
They were young men, conscripted and spiced
with a taste of Zionist venom. They eyed him with
disquiet, a distrust of the outsider. One yelped:
'Stop, no nearer.'
'I come form Africa with the wisdom of a Primal
Gene and that infinity of the Serpent. The true
essence of Jesus of Nazareth is held in these
scrolls I carry.' One of the soldiers addressed his
confederates: 'Another one who thinks he's
Jesus.' 'Come back to save us all.' replied his
mate. A soldier crunched towards him: 'If you're so
high and mighty stop this.' A rifle butt crashed
across his back: 'How about that. Still think you're
Jesus?' 'A real nutter' A sergeant intervened: 'Now
lads...better get him to the loony bin.' And sand
blew across the soldiers' check point and their
eyes were smarted. At the hospital Dr. Rue sat
down in a small, white-washed room. He was
rotund with whispery blond hair, which was so fine
it appeared to be gossamer in nature. 'Well you
nearly got yourself shot. Those soldiers are
trained to shoot fast first and no questions asked.'
'I am the bearer of wisdom.' 'Yes. Is it esoteric?' 'It
can only be disseminated to the few and then
must be preached globally.' 'And whom...?' 'The
burden of truth upon me is so much.' 'What's in
your bag?' 'The Truth is in the scrolls.' 'I am a
spiritual man, do you think I could, under your
supervision, read the scrolls?' 'There is a yoke of
burden upon my shoulders, it is the weight of

enlightenment.' The room hummed with expectation as the psychiatrist prepared for the usual Majnoon delusions. Was the young man just another Majnoon? He began: 'I was handed these scrolls by a young women, she wore rags and had a certain presence, a charisma about her. She named me much to my astonishment and told me to head for Jerusalem. There I should gather a group of those who are spiritually and socially illegitimate. She gave me these scrolls and strolled into the distance without another word. A sense of mission enfolded my body with comforting warmth, my spirit was exalted. So that is how I achieved enlightenment, a brief encounter with an effervescent girl whose eyes were like purple light.' He took the scrolls from his bag and began to speak the text which they contained: 'This is the truth about Jesus of Nazareth. Three wandering teachers in a quest for illumination were travelling through Africa in search for its ancient knowledge, Africa being the cradle of civilization and a land of fertility. As the sun rose and awoke these mystics, they perceived a golden matrix. Slowly they approached and became aware of dancing purple lights. They had stumbled or been lead to the Oracle who spoke of her sister the Primal Gene which is the source of humanity. Having located the precise spot, they unearthed an urn shrouded in a golden fleece. The oracle then caressed them with the wisdom to carry the urn to its appointed place and the knowledge of the precise moment to break the seals. It directed them to Palestine. Mary, a quiet girl of 13, had spent the sun beamed day looking after a moderate sized flock of lazy sheep. Running home she felt warmth of weariness and settled down to rest on show straw in a barn. Three itinerant mystics, hungry and thirsty, saw purple light drifting around the barn. The lights were intense and confronted the teachers. It became immediately clear that at location they should break employ the ancient law and break the bejewelled jar. They entered the barn and while Mary was asleep, they carefully broke the seals on the urn and then gently fertilised her with the Primal Gene. This was in accordance with he wishes of the Oracle, that ancient law. She awoke with a sense of unutterable tranquillity. As the months passed it became clear that she was pregnant. Joseph, her boy-friend, decided to marry Mary to remove any social stain which others would besmirch them with. The boy child was born in a shower of purple droplets. Jesus was illegitimate having been conceived outside marriage. Jesus was a reticent and pensive child who preferred solitude to the games of other children. As a youth he was bullied by other boys because he was illegitimate. On one occasion Jesus saw flashing purple lights and these animated with an authority as old as Africa and he said: 'I am the illegitimate One who draws everyone who is also illegitimate in any way to his side, I take you into my heart'. The others thought this weird but some regarded him as enigmatic and stopped the bullying.

   Mary understood her son's serpent. The serpent swallows itself eternally and therefore creates an infinite circle where it consumes itself: good and evil consume each other for infinity. But Jesus realized these concepts were all rooted in the material, he realized there was a bio-chemical basis for these phenomenon. Upon this epiphany Jesus was Transfigured, the primal gene within exploded and he was wrapped in a cloak of purple. His body and mind were vibrating with an explosive ecstasy. Surrounded by veils of purple he began to each. Hr spoke in parables and with an intensity which captivated his congregations. Banished from the synagogue, he wandered with a core of disciples. He said: 'I am the primal gene, the alpha of humanity.' And again 'My gene is your gene, I am within you.' Once he said: 'I am you and you are me.' He taught: 'As my heart beats so does yours.' Jesus made his journey complete by travelling to Jerusalem. Banishing his disciples he entered the Garden of Gethsemane, the Garden of History and was alone except for his purple lights for company. He prepared to discover the quintessential nature of his destiny, the primal genes sparked within. His contemplation, a barbed introspection became so intense he sweated blood. He sighed: 'I am wisdom incarnate and it is stroking every strand of my hair. I am the illegitimate one and I bring socio-political illegitimacy to its fruition.' Jesus now knew is destiny, he would became a sacrifice for the Zealots who were revolutionaries opposing both the Jewish establishment and the Roman occupiers. The Jewish ruling class with the notable exception of Joseph of Aramethea had conspired to put Jesus on trail and have him executed by the Roman colonial power. Jesus was subsequently arrested and found guilty of sedition. But as he was being handed over to Pilot, the Roman Governor, a purple splinter cut into his mind and he drew out a dagger from his cloak and assassinated Pilot shouting: 'I am history, History will vindicate me.' Will in the dock for the murder of Pilot he said: 'The trail of the illegitimate one is the trail of the Zealots and consequently you will deal with the people. I am he people incarnate. My wisdom is their Wisdom. I leave the people in tumult, but weep not for true revelation is incarnate in my chosen Zealots. Their path is immaculate struggle'. Jesus is taken to a quiet place and nailed to a cross. Hanging he ejaculates:

'In leaving I remain, I am the DNA of the masses, in this illegitimacy I gather all those who weep in my heart.'

 Dr Rue inhaled: 'Fascinating.

' The reply: 'Do you believe?'

Dr Rue whispers: 'You have the Divine Madness, go in peace Majnoon.'

George Orwell's '1984': revisited.

Winston Smith and Julia had been banished by Big Brother to a sandy and wind-swept wilderness. Here their flesh was burnt by the relentless sun and their hunger only assuaged by a love which transcended the abysmal curse of the 'Thought-Police'. Bodies almost too raw to touch, they made love with a deep and dark energy which came from a liberated libidinal drive. They had penetrated deep into the Id and like a hurricane that came from their essences banished all banality, intoxicating with interacting unconsciousness'. Other exiles had struggled and heaved their way across the shifting desert and torn themselves on its obscured rocks. Their feet were cut and bruised as they climbed into incrustations which provided temporary shelter from the blazing sun. These exiles had been drawn from the various strata of the 'Outer Party'. Some accused of tarnishing the purity of 'Newspeak'. Others cast-out for sexual activity which was banned for them and, yet, others for keeping clandestine journals. Big Brother had cast these outsiders into this harsh terrain from where there was no apparent return only after they had been 'de-cultured' and professed their love for Big Bother. Torture had been used until they 'confessed' to their crimes; Electro Convulsive Therapy had been employed as one method to extract these so-called revelations. Then processed in the 'Ministry of Love' they had been accessed as being rehabilitated and therefore needed no further treatment and where cast, apparently broken, into the wilderness. Gradually they had melted into the night like roaming pariahs, but they left sighs like all scavengers, and they began to locate each other and form into little bands, almost packs. These groups moved in an every reducing circle until they began to coalesce. When this jell had formed it was inevitable that Winston and Julia would become a beacon, because of their intellectual and erotic challenge to Big Brother and his apparatus the 'Thought Police'. They would guide their comrades through the bitter nights of wilderness and isolation. But passivity began to pervade the group, choking it like a hang-man's noose. Winston and Julia left the group saying:

'We may be gone a little while, its important ideological work, remember love and solidarity.' They wandered into the wilderness guided by the anti-Father, the antithesis of Big Brother who was the collective memory of Goldstein. They were drawn to a ragged cliff and climbed until exhausted they had reached a crevice hidden by brush. Within lay pure white tablets of stone about the size of a volume of Marx/Engels 'Selected Works', delving into the aperture they found three, a trinity. On their return other members of the group or as they were now calling themselves: 'Revolutionary Proletarian Cell', for Winston had said long ago: 'If there is hope it lies in the proles.' Upon these stones Winston and Julia, employing the instruments devised by their brothers and sisters, their comrades, began to give tangible form to their abstract thoughts and their physical experiences. It read, indeed proclaimed: '1) Only the proletariat can overthrow the Party and Big Brother. This is the product of our objective analysis and is our goal 2) We do not know what the subjective conditions are within the proletarian zones, by that we mean there is no awareness of the consciousness of the proletariat, their class consciousness. 3) Consequently the 'Cell' must adopt the tactic of infiltration into the sealed proletarian zones. The zones of the lost, who by their own activity shall, be found as a class. 4) Any means necessary is, ultimately, justified by the achievement of the ends.' After a number of forages across the wasteland to the workers ghettos, they obtained essential items such as worker's clothes. Gradually they accumulated a collection of items, bits and pieces and like a circling eagle reconnoitred the terrain before swooping on its prey, but the masses weren't the prey , they were the instrument to be employed against the prey. Like the dawn wipes the tyranny of night from the world the 'Cell' began what they believed and had interpreted from Engels as their: 'World historic mission.' As twilight began to dissolve the colours of day they penetrated the worker's zone; then were confronted with an ink black smog which was almost Dickensian and the neglected tower-blocks where the masses existed with the horrors of a life separated from its meaning, its essence, but the 'Cell' would help create this essence even if it required destroying the existential to allow the essence to have a vehicle to articulate itself, allowing the masses to emancipate themselves. Winston and Julia now rested from the 'Cell's period of wandering, assumed the everyday running of their group. Everywhere the belching of factories and the preparations for yet more wars in which the workers would be sacrificed to the insane logic of Big Brother created a terrain of ideological anaemia as well as poverty. The people seemed to walk bent over under the yoke of alienation and be shackled to the hopeless grind of their lives. their intellectual and cultural diet, force-feed, was a combination of sentimentality and pornography which, in totality, had lead to a soporific and subservient proletariat. Winston was despondent: 'How can we organize or ignite these people it's like the task of Sisyphus. All is lost.' Julia replied: 'Let us travel beyond appearance into essence, we may be surprised what we discover find.' The 'Cell' conducted a collective analysis after all had reported back to Winston and Julia their experiences of the 'class' atomized and suffering from state sponsored Banalism and the 'line' was agreed. Julia and Winston would emerge into the masses and try and find some, any, tool of disrupting the sickness of the proletariat. The others would behave as invisible revolutionaries awaiting the call to action.

The moved, almost staggered through the proletarian zones only to be met with blank smiles or vacuous grimaces. Days heaved into weeks and it was becoming like a razor-blade before a suicide attempt. It appeared that the labouring masses were, to all intents and purposes dead, certainly unresponsive to anything than the 'Party's' constant stream of platitudes and patriotism. Eventually they entered the central areas; here there were just shacks, dismal hovels. Julia suddenly smiled and said: 'It is here that the wound is at its most rancid. It is here where the depths of the oppressed are to be found.' With a trembling sense of trepidation and expectation Julia and Winston approached one of hovels. They knocked on the flimsy but heavily chained door. A head, well a skull with deep blackened sockets peered around the edge: 'What yer want...best smack we got, ten quid a bag ... blow yer away.' Julia answered in the language she had learnt in an 'Outer Party' manual of 'prolespeak.' 'Cool, we can score here.' 'Yea baby...got any works.' An emaciated figure unshackled the door and said:

'Best shooting gallery in town man.'

Winston and Julia entered this palace of despair, quivering. A man, the 'Man', sat in a haze of tangerine; his eyes seemed like amber jewels glaring like furnaces in the gloom of the shooting gallery. He hovered out of the door leaving the two revolutionaries and the skeletal worker. He groaned: 'Do you up for that other ten quid bag. Just do my business first.' Julia and Winston looked in horror as he slithered up his shirtsleeve, arms covered in needle marks, bruises and seeping abscesses. He searched pathetically for a vein that wasn't just an inflamed track: 'Got a hit...far out man... ahhrrr cool stuff.' The junkie was how in a haze and flushing blood and water in and out of his syringe, sucking it and squirting it into cracked white mug. Immediately with the force of a passion released from the unconscious by a lover Julia and Winston became aware that this polluted blood with its dream serum was the agent of social transformation. The 'Cell' gathered in the depths of the inner zones and a new line was, this time, enforced by the revolutionary couple on their comrades: 'We had believed that only through the rise in class consciousness and a consequent proletarian revolution could Big Brother, or to be more accurate comrades Big Daddy, can be removed. However it has become apparent it is only through the dissemination of decadence and hedonism particularly through i.v. drug use that the system can be undermined, if not overthrown. This pollution must happen from the base to the pinnacle...only in this way can the next generation be cleansed and emancipated. You remember the ends justify the means by any necessary praxis.' Julia continued: 'Hence decadence contains in itself the apotheosis of the masses.' Winston concluded: 'It is necessary to spread an immorality, almost a plague, it will eventually consume the Party in its entirety and Big Brother Himself. And from these ruins will raise proto communism.' During the next day/nights the 'Cell' fuelled by what was becoming a contorted, almost distorted, zeal, they spread hard drugs and whatever other encouragement was necessary to propagate the new line. Making money and then investing, reinvesting; wasn't this a little like the cycle of Capital accumulation discovered by Marx? However workers became too ill to work regularly and the Gross Domestic Product began to fall, the destruction of the masses was being used for the emancipation of the masses: to destroy 'double-think', well that's what the 'Cell' had come to believe. They had been in the wilderness so long they had lost touch of their own philosophical concepts; these had become hopeless abstractions without a base in the material, in reality, in the masses. But Big

Brother's war-drive finally collapsed and with it the dynamic of His system. Intravenous heroin use became endemic within the 'Inner Party' which was already disintegrating because of factional struggles. Suddenly with the combination of economic failure and a structural crisis in the leadership in the ruling class the 'Cell' (they hadn't made any attempt to recruit members to their group) saw their strategy had proven successful. The problem was though they had destroyed the structure of the system they had also weakened the only force that could replace it; the proletariat. Mistakenly they had believed that an almost sacrificial plague, the immolation of and by the masses through the spreading of dissolute habits and practices was the solution, but it was not. One morning Julia and Winston stumbled upon a building where the 'tele-screen' was still working, but only just...it was a grey blurred haze with a figure that seemed spectral. They realized it was a dim image of Big Brother. He said solemnly and in a measured tone: 'This is the final analysis. We have reached Omega, therefore the Inner Party has dissolved itself. History and hence Reason or sanity has been concluded. The only option for me is...' He slowly eased a revolver from the desk he was sitting behind: 'Too create my own myth.' He placed the revolved in his month and the 'tele-screen' pang into darkness. As the next few years past a semblance of order returned to society. Methods for treating the previous socio-cultural problems were successfully created and implemented. Julia mused: 'Could Humanity really taste it's essence in these conditions, isn't the freedom for self-destruction a much deeper drive than socio-economic drives.' She realized Big Brother, Big Daddy was just an image from her unconscious, and she had destroyed the symbol of the father from whom she never received love. She grasped a kitchen-knife and in a deliberate and potent act stabbed herself in the heart. But rumours were now beginning to spread. Had Big Brother really committed suicide for the 'tele-screen' had blanked out at the vital moment? Had Big Brother really fled with some close 'Inner Party' comrades into the wilderness as Winston and Julia had years before?

Did all this really happen or was it a ghastly delusion projected by some expelled members of the 'Inner Party' which had led to Julia's suicide? Only you can decide.

The Prank.

The student bar was jumping with youthful
drunkenness. Ian enjoyed this apparently
harmless pleasure. However, as he walked a little
unsteadily to the bar, Jake, who was known for his
ability or vocation to obtain mind-altering drugs,
slipped a crunched micro-dot of LSD into Ian's
beer. Jake muttered: 'This will give him God'. I
should explain that Ian was reading 19th History
and had discovered that strain of dissent to the
march of industrial Capital called 'Evangelism'.
While he didn't practice he was aware and had
spoken of the intense spiritual experiences
claimed by those while being converted. It was
late and Ian had begun to feel a little peculiar. He
noticed a vibration inside his skull. Focussing on
reaching his room and with a great grey mist
hovering above managed to close the door to his
room with huge relief. Time and space seemed to
be melting into the walls. He could hear colours,
surely this was madness. Then an exquisite beam
of limelight shone room a gulping mouth in the
ceiling. As this humming beam of joy approached
Ian felt the most unutterable peace that penetrated
his head, the most sublime ecstasy. This could
only be a conversion experience he thought, it
was like the accounts he'd read on the History
module. A Bible on his bookshelf became alight
with 'tongues of fire', indeed he appeared able to
speaking tongues, was this the 'gift of the Holy
Spirit.'. About six hours later as the L.S.D. wore off
Ian became convinced he'd had a profound
religious experience. You must remember he was
unaware that his beer had been adulterated with

L.S.D. Dawn rose and its tentacles strangled the last of the hallucinations and Ian who felt purged slipped into his bed and dozed. As the sleep caressed his inner most depths the idea of his mission began to congeal in Ian's mind. He spent the morning with a sense of being purged and became convinced he must evangelise. He realized his transformation in him would be recognized by other students but didn't think they would be any adverse consequences; he was a man of vision and they were blind the he believed. During the next weeks Ian's desire for food diminished, he paced the campus with eyes like fire and most shrunk away and avoided him. Ian believed this was a natural reaction to his elevated state of awareness, for isn't a prophet always shunned by his contemporaries. A young woman named Anna, unlike most others, wondered how such a transformation could have overtaken Ian. She was drawn by his intensity and his increasingly ragged appearance intrigued her; she was curious. Over the next three weeks their conversations became more and more intense. Anna finally said: 'How you suddenly changed, you were such a diligent student, I'm not sure who you are?' You seem to wrap me in the warmth that I only remember as a small child, being held by my parents. You ease my emotions, being different, not like one of the other students. I feel made whole by you, are you, please don't misunderstand me but I came from a Christian background, but are you the Chosen One...?' She blushed and fell down inside, had she revealed too much of herself. Ian sat like a crumbling statue, he was unshaven and brown hair hung helplessly in a mass of greasy sprigs. Trembling he replied: 'I am the prophet and you are the prophetess. You are an incarnation of the 19th century prophetess Joanna Southall. We are together, our souls and bodies will intertwine in a frenzy of divine love. Our child, he or she will lead those who are of the Light to their kingdom of God... this will be in the New Jerusalem which is to be established on earth.' They held each other in a sparking aura of orange mist, the child was conceived, and their sighs seem to pulse with the beat of nature. Exhausted they slept in each in each other's arms, but once madness is fanned it can become a raging blaze. The gossip began to wind its way through campus like a vine of ivy. Jake thought: 'What have I done? It was a prank, a joke but now he's insane. It is my fault.' Jake was brimming with remorse. In his box of tricks from which he had conjured the L.S.D. that had spiked Ian's drink there was a syringe and several grams of amphetamine. He cooked-up and with a steady hand and wrote: 'I am full of remorse, so sorry to have ruined Ian's life and that of his weird girlfriend. Put some drugs in his drink. Can't life with the guilt. Mum and dad, am so sorry.' By the time Jake had committed suicide Ian and Anna were living in a tent and roaming the countryside. They lived a nomadic life until Anna went into premature labour. Between them they managed to persuade a very wary person to drive them to the nearest hospital. The nurses were shocked at their dishevelled appearance, their dirty hair and clothes. The labour was intense, but the baby was stillborn. Anna was to be kept in hospital for several days while Ian was given a shower and a solid meal. He was in a state of shock and then wondered: 'Why, why? Our child was to beacon which would banish darkness and now he is dead, my God, dead.' He was devastated and a tidal wave began to destroy any rational analysis that might have remained since his 'trip' and involvement with Anna, the floods of worthlessness followed by dark whirling pools of self-hatred, a mental crucifixion of his mind followed. If she had been provided with the proper care during the last few months, the child might have lived. He would rather have died than the child should have been born dead. Ian left, then roamed until he found a pub were he could buy drugs, the language of the 'scene' was becoming to have an assonance with him, he had 'scored'. He emerged from the pub with an assortment of 'downers' for oblivion seekers. Ian was functioning on automatic now. He bought a large bottle of lemonade and walked from the town into the countryside. His one perceived aim – self destruction. This he thought in a distorted ay would compensate the World for the 'sacrifice' of their child who they believed would have been Divine. Totally focused on the child's death and his failings...Anna was outside the orbit of his awareness. He sat with his back to a hedgerow and began o stuff handfuls of tranquilizers into his mouth and washed them down with lemonade. An hour later he was unconscious and drifting towards death. Fortune intervened and a farm worker stumbled upon Ian, he was close to death. Ian had no recollection of his stomach being pumped and the days in an Intensive Care Unit. Slowly he gained wakefulness and became aware of the numerous tubes and pipes in and around his body. As day followed day Ian left the Intense Care ward. Within a week his strength was returning as a sponge draws in liquid and gradually he began to ponder the future. Then one day a doctor appeared who was not dressed in a white coat unlike the other doctors: 'Hello Ian' he said in a tranquil voice. 'How are you feeling?' Ian replied 'Stronger.' 'Do you have any thoughts or ideas about your unique spiritual nature?' 'How do you know anything about my beliefs?' The doctor smiled: 'We've spoken to your girlfriend.' 'Ann, she would not say that she is a prophetess. 'We're enlightened parents of a child who would take people from darkness to light.' The psychiatrist replied: 'Okay, have you ever taken LSD?' 'No, no absolutely not.' You had a friend called Jake, I'm afraid to say he died, but in a note admitted to spiking your beer with L.S.D.' Ian exploded: 'I don't believe that, I was chosen by God, not some drug dealer.' Dr. Guy replied: 'Right, I'm going to give you some medicine.' Ian shouted; 'You fool, I don't want your potions, I'm leaving hospital soon anyway'.

Dr. Guy smiled again and walked briskly away. Ian thought there could be trouble here. Soon a pack of nurses arrived with a cardboard plate with a brown ampoule and a plastic syringe. Ian panicked and screamed; 'What are you going to do to me?' The male nurse coldly replied: 'Just something to make you feel comfortable, Oh, by the way, if you're thinking of refusing treatment don't, you've been detained under the Mental Health Act. You are going to be given compulsory medication, don't resist.' Ian cried aloud; 'You are the forces of darkness...' 'Now, we don't want any tantrums, do we? You can have it the simply or the hard way and you will remember it for a long time.' Four nurses held Ian on the bed. Struggling was useless now. One said: 'There's a good lad.' And he jammed the needle into Ian's buttock. 'Just what the doctor ordered, Ian.'

Ian soon felt a chemical drowsiness and plunged, like diving into an ocean of pitch black, into a deep sleep. When he awoke here were two male nurses sitting on chairs at the bottom of his bed. One spoke: 'Oh, God's woken up.' The other said menacingly; 'You're coming up the Hill with us.' Ian realized that is was a reference to a mental hospital. Still in hospital issue pyjamas and dressing gown, a drowsy Ian was bundled into an ambulance with the nurses. He moaned: 'Thought police'. The response: 'Quiet, now you don't want to be a difficult lad, do you?' Ian stuttered: 'You have not experienced the Sublime.' 'Look Ian, you can either make this stay easy or we can teach you a lesson, it's up to you. And we don't want any more of this prophet business. We can make your life easy or tough, it's your choice.' He was heavily sedated for several weeks, his memory weak, his thoughts paralysed, and he felt generally leaden. In fact, he spent most of this early part of his admission asleep. Nurse would say: 'No trouble now, just some syrup to make you feel your old self.' Ian's medication was gradually reduced. He began to wonder what his 'old self' had been. Bewildered he wandered the corridors of Ward 10, with its floors of regimented tiled floors and cream walls. The ward sister said: 'The next step is for you to go on a ten-minute escorted walk around the grounds. Clare will be with you. Remember, no antics, you're still on a section and we don't want any performances, do we Ian.' Ian quietly consented. As the next few weeks went by Ian's walks with Clare became longer and longer. Having explored the undulating grassy lawns, walked around the ivory clad long-stay wards and the many trees which seemed like old and reassuring friends in the grounds, they began to set out for the cornfields and beyond. Clare would talk about the nature of religious experience. Ian was cautious about and fairly resistant to these conversations. But as the months travelled into autumn, he began to understand that his drink had been spiked. Clare went step by step through Ian's experiences on that fateful night. She compared LSD experiences and drug induced psychosis with spiritual experiences. Gradually she showed him that it was possible to re-build his life. Dr. Guy was busy, cancelling Ian's twelve-month section and putting him on a cocktail of less sedating drugs. With the encouragement of Clare Ian was banishing, coming out of his psychosis. He began to feel warmth in her presence and noticed her brown air, always a little untidy but this attracted him. Her aura seemed to him to be one of compassion and wisdom. He was falling in love. As the illness was evaporated by her sun, that same sun kindled his desire. It was now winter, and Ian was to be returned to he community and hopefully to university for the next academic year. Clare and Ian, as part of the rehabilitation programme, had been buying clothes and books. They were sitting in a café with two hot mugs of tea in their hands, Ian slid is hand, so his fingertips brushed Clare's. He then began lightly stroking her blushing cheeks:

'I love you with all my heart, my feelings whirl around me when we are close. You are my life, my love sweet Clare.'

She began to weep softly:

'Ian, I am sorry, but there is something you must know. I was a nun. I took vows of obedience, poverty and poor Ian, chastity. I broke the vow of obedience by leaving the convent but have maintained the other two vows. We could ever have a relationship other than friendship. You will return to everyday life, fall for a girl, and fall in love. I am sorry...' She dried her eyes:

'That is not my path.'

Ian felt numb: 'I suppose to quote Lawrence 'we are crucified by desire.'

Clare replied: 'It need not be like that Ian...'

Oedipus resurrects his mother and they roam suburbia

'Writing sustains me and a non-writing writer is, in fact, a monster courting insanity
- Franz Kafka.

This flame had burnt before the Apple was bit, the Lamb does not take away the sin of the World but stitches with the thread of the Oracle, and the son is Blinded, he is an anti-Lamb, the lost sheep, that wolf who roams and is guided by nothing but the sweet scent of blood in the Sacrament it is unblemished in a vial which hangs around his furry neck, those eyes which offended had been plucked-out many feverish tossed nights ago at Calvary: 'the King is dead, the Queen is dead, long live Oedipus' chants a priest without vestments within the rubble of that defiled temple overgrown by the willow which choked, clasped and entrapped in old asylums: be alert now the coffin lid is to be lifted and the thorns, the razor thorns and spikes of the dead queen's uncut, mould covered distortedly curled nails glint sharp, better beware our resurrection is not to be subdued by that bell nor the driving in of a stake, these risen lovers are to be reborn in their own womb of dark red beds of crinkled-up rose petals coloured by her crimson blood, black like her son's. 'Some of you show supposed shock. The poet is buried and mummified in linen of innuendo with the stigmata stain, this is nothing, but your own heaven and hell married and marred, you aren't Vaguely surprised.' Mother was in a plugged blue glass bottle but he pulled the cork. They dig and shuffle and grasp hand over hand

the dirt from the graves in Which some entombed
them, the mauve and green termites do swarm
inward. Oedipus and Jocasta are not destined to
wander a rustic idyll, the shepherds Left long ago,
but they will roam silent suburban sprawls
spewing forth worms which dig deeply in eyes like
maggots eating rotten apples, this terrible taste?

'Beware the green-eyed monster.'

At Time's gestation there was pure ovulation in the fathomless Void. It was as the first Apple was given and bitten that the 'green-eyed one's' were conceived, they have and will try and throw the poet into a pit of noxious fumes, these people believe they are on the mission like latter-day Jesuits, but beware if you're not a passive sheep or even worse if you are a Steppenwolf pulling a sledge of books and papers across an urban wasteland, they fear and abhor you, watch out if you have the audacity to write with that brown burnt disc which is the sun which they have never seen nor have plunged into, beware if it gets into print: 'they will persist with that publication; oh it all rather gives us a heavy migraine', dazed hooded-eyed hawks yours are atrophied appendixes to texts dreamt of yet were not to be written, these Fiends are smitten because they bit juicy Apple of power, it is nothing but fruit which fell from the Tree and lays there oozing maggots, so poisoned and intoxicated there are those who believe they have some elevated knowledge like a wealthy pauper, mechanized privileged perception, some are called priests, there are others who masquerade as doctors of Reason and more who just worm there way into the ruined asylums, all are without compassion just irrationality transmogrified into quasi- science, it was said by Marx that 'the philosophers have interpreted the world the point is however to change it' by the one who dreamt of dialectics, a dancer gliding on the spectrum of synthesised Absolutes, just evoked rainbows from an undulating mass of poets who knew not that they were poets, the yoked, the workers, women and peasants who await with their fountain pen to gush resplendent and then they will write exquisite script across the unravish'd page, the Fall will then be renounced, the Tree will blossom with the poems written by its roots. You pound the nails with the thud, thud of your hammering-myths into the palms of an anonymous poets; yes, you inflict that horrid pain yet still blood trickles onto the index-finger and your ignominy is to be scratched on parchments of stars. Beware do not open our bejewelled Pandora's Box which is our play-crate, because you do not know our pure beauty, our stone gaze which is so terrible it would ossify the oceans.

Note. 'O! Beware, my lord, of jealously, it is the green-eyed monster.' Shakespeare: 'Othello'.

A priestly vocation?

'Two souls, alas, are housed within my breast, and each will wrestle for the mastery there'. - Goethe.

After a troubled and largely sleepless night Peter the priest scuttled like a frightened insect out of his room. The dreams are becoming a little too intense and seem to merge into wakefulness, Holy Mother of God, the madness isn't returning, I beg you he muttered, I've got to give it up: the smack. His skin was no longer young, not a fresh page on which to scribe poetry to the grandeur of God who had been his fountainhead in the early years, but alternatively not the wrinkled dried criss-crossed dried parchment of an old man awaiting his wake. Jesus of the Holy Blood I need a hit of you, of that first time I celebrated the Holy Mass, what joy, unadulterated beauty. But now the immaculate blood was not in the silver chalice he raised with extreme care to a line above his forehead for his meagre bunch of communicates to genuflect before. Oh yes mainly hypocrites and deceivers, a real bunch of Pharisees, one or two he had high hopes for. Even madman John was in the latter group, 'no reason you cannot fulfil your vocation to the ideals of Saint Francis of Assisi.' What happened, preserve us all, he began shoplifting and giving away the loot to those street-addicts in the poor quarter. Yes that was a place for a priest to minister, but not to have their brown and white powders and those hellish off-white crystals administered to madman John or anyone else, particularly myself I had thought. I genuinely believed we, us, the flock at Mass were different to those skeletal, emaciated creatures with taunt yellowing shin pulled around sunken eyes, those deep black hollows, those empty eyes, my God. That was almost three years ago now and my, our, understanding of what was meant by the immaculate would be transformed; indeed, our bodies and souls would be transmogrified.

Peter was quick to pull on his baggy black priestly uniform which covered and gave some volume to a meagre frame, the rest he explained by his devotion to fasting. But then the cold would burrow, almost bit, like a pulsating, squirming pile of purple worms and claw, eat into his body which would then whiplash into some kind of sweat which seemed like a tropical fever. He knew that the mainline to the Divine was not the one recommended by his spiritual director, who he assiduously avoided, but the immaculate track which is marked by those stigmata which were nothing but regular neat lines of needle marks. Mass was at six fifteen, he had to straighten-out for that, but he could not celebrate that Mass, for those who attended so early where the real zealots and had the attentiveness of your average drug-squad officer, he pondered. What was the remedy? He knew only too well, it smashed through his skull into that tormented brain, of course there was nothing to worry about; he had stashed a little 'brown' away and with a couple or three tablets of diazepam he would be fit again, perhaps not celebrate the mass, but manage some kind of automated performance without his fingers becoming purple appendages of his hands fiddling feebly and trembling in a fumble out from his vestments.

I rummage around under the sink, thank God, here's the stash. Unravel the brown paper in a flurry of hands, yes all that's required is here, praise be to whom, I wonder to God or to the Man? Certainly not madman John suddenly I am temporary disorientated. 'No need to worry he'll 'get through' okay'. Disengaged from the surrounding world I fall back into the tedium of the business at hand, how many years now, yes that's right three and it will be soon be Easter.' Peter, with the precision of a locksmith, smoothed the silver paper, manoeuvres, with the assistance of a razor-blade a line of brown powder that within a minute or two will sooth the creases from his mind. The 'line' of brown powder is straight down the middle of the foil which he holds left-handed. Inserted into his quivering lips is a cone, itself constructed of silver foil, but carefully, lovely, compulsively fashioned by his fleshless and claw like fingers into a utensil of pleasure, which has now become an instrument of necessity. In his right hand is an orange plastic lighter. He raises the left hand which holds the foil to within about four centimetres of the cone, ignites the lighter, a click, and with the swift yet careful movement of hand a flame scolds the silver foil; almost caressing it. The line of inanimate brown heroin bubbles into life, becomes suddenly a liquid then and finally, until the next time he 'chases the dragon', it becomes vapour. He inhales from right to left in one breath, then a pull from an already ignited cigarette...warmth engulfs his mind, then a womb-like peace enshrouds him. Finally he exhales stumbles and sits down. 'Not the mainline to the divine, but will be adequate until later on'. The tumbler of water is lifted, the three yellow tablets of diazepam swallowed. 'Give me half an hour and I'll be steady as the rock upon which the Church is built', he whispers playfully. A series of waves which are like frenzied screeches resound through his mind: 'madman John how are you, where are you, who are you?' He is startled and gathers his paraphernalia agitatedly, but with the paradox of addiction smoothly into the plastic bag which he places and wraps it in brown paper, then his stash is safe.

Mass passed fairly uneventfully, a combination of him being comfortably numb and the single track spirituality of the 6.15ers who knew the Mass so well it was less a ritual than memorized piece of text which they'd pattered out for years, a sort of rapid mindless muttering. The next act of evasion consisted in avoiding the Parish Priest, the boss in the presbytery, and the housekeeper, a devout woman but with a soul of iron at breakfast. His deceptions and manipulations were almost the same length of his habit, the cassock which dragged through this benumbed ministry of distorting mirrors; the reflections were becoming more grotesque day by day. This had began, it seemed now through an opiated haze, with those series of acts 'downtown' with madman John, who had in many ways Peter pondered was the incarnation of the Franciscan ethic plus; plus what? The psychiatric nurses who would periodically whisk him into what remained of the local mental hospital, much of it lay derelict; care-in-the-community, seemed madman John didn't receive any 'meaningful' care, at best Peter would use the term management to describe it. What care did either of them really get, but chemical care? Plus, what? The question bounced around his mind like a rubber ball; they had said schizophrenia, but, the priest cogitated, madman John has that simplicity, no that's the wrong word, that purity of a rejection of the world which was a central tenet, at least it should be Peter thought, of the Franciscan ethic. Then it hit him like the locomotive of History, Trotsky had mentioned it he seemed to recall from his seminary days, which was Revolution, put more succinctly 'cold turkey', he was beginning to withdraw. Had to get downtown and quickly, the clams were beginning to attach themselves to his mind and the leeches to his cold moist flesh.

'Father, Father Peter, stop its John. I've been baptising near the river. I'm John the Baptist.
' Holy shit thought the priest; he's really lost it this time and I need a hit.'
'Don't worry Father; it's not full immersion, rather the intravenous administration of pharmaceutical diamorphine.'
'Thank God.'
'It will soon be Easter Father, so I thought we'd better resurrect some of these downtown Lazarus people. St. Peter told me himself. You yourself Father Peter.'
'John you child, I'm not a saint, I'm a junkie.'
John: 'We have one last hit, the immaculate hit, I've got the ampoules here.' 'Perhaps there is something of Peter in me, I've denied my Master and my vocation far more than three times. There is no mainline to paradise John, we make that or

not here on Earth and that is a dreadful burden, an awful freedom. John, madman John, let us drink deeply from the streams within our hearts. That is human blood; the sacred blood which all breasts pound with and their hearts have no masters.'

And with this they unbound the funereal bandages from their arms and legs and grasped each other tight. There's like all the other downtown Lazarus people was not an easy path, but had not the priest's guru spoken of the 'narrow gait', perhaps pondered the priest, it is only us, those like Lazarus who have experienced death in all its manifestations that can comprehend it:

John said: 'What about the ampoules Father, why waste them.'

A wry smile came over the gaunt face and exposed his yellow teeth:

 'Well one for the road, just to say good-bye to it all.'

They were found blue with the blood congealing in their syringes. It was so simple; they had forgotten to reduce the dosage for this was pharmaceutical heroin, not street gear, not Lazarus gear.

Was that just a...dream?

Rattlesnake in the mind of the passenger of the red-bus, Midland Red bus, rolls past the Red house, where he was sent by the Party, but lost the argument on the nature of the Soviet Union with a solitary, in many ways, shop steward. Peter the steward, who sat like a 'desert-rat' about to chisel away at the statue of Ozymandias behind a poorly vanished square table occasionally taking sips from a single whisky, it would take him exactly an hour to consecrate this small tumbler made of thick glass, then the next. The wizardry of words took place, over many, many evenings, but it was John from the 4th International who had cast the spell, the most potent of all the enchantment of ideas. The passenger sits coiled in faded blue jeans of a generation wandering to ...'try to concentrate that those other people on the bus do exist as matter....' The veil was lifted on another trip which had burnt out his eyes like acid only to reveal other landscapes, looking deeper into fathomless ocean within, hopeless holes of introspection which he fell through. People begin to inhale and exhale, lets breath, gulp in one great gush of oxygen. Did the passenger just say: 'Am I breathing?'

No it was that lizard sitting opposite. There are two rows of sets huddled into this rectangle crate called a bus, divided by a two foot gangway which has a matt black covering worn by the interminable daily journeys of these people, back and forth, going and coming. Are they really sitting in a glasshouse and, he thinks, should I throw a couple of stones; But then just mumbles into his hand: 'Wake up your predators, just spit out your poison'. The bus is travelling along a channel, a grove worn by journeys that shudder through the grid of a town and then winds through equally ordered suburban excuses for those who think they belong, but none belong here…Wham! Was that green, not lawn manicured, but grass really unapologetically muddy in winter, fine like a young man's dawn in spring, strong and thick as a women's at the zenith of her lunar arch and stiff with frost at the ache of her going to sleep. I woke up and almost fell out of the door of that can on four rather worn looking tyres while it was cruising away, it wasn't wreaked but then neither was I. Not 'stoned' that is, but dreamy and floating. Had that nightmare ended last night, the last incarnation of a flea? He glanced at the pavement; yes, the cracks seem to have attained the status of the chequered symmetry of a chessboard. I drifted away, the cracks had now become caverns in the rumble which I was walking through, above and below simultaneously, a kind of marriage of heaven and hell, most stop reading Blake at the moment. Certainly, round the corner of the first detached, red-bricked house in this little street is a precipice who begs you to throw yourself over into a ravine of distorted faces whose eyes weep into each other.

 'You weirdo', 'Hippie scum' 'Loony commie', you …'
'What did you say, mother-fuckers?'
'You heard, fresh out of the nuthouse again?
The jeers had come from a group of lads who were vaguely approaching puberty and haven't quite managed the transition walking past the

entrance of the red-bricked street. I grasp hold of
a tablet of stone deep within me upon which is
written in indelible ink; 'the proletariat is the agent
of social transformation.' But some seem
particularly alienated. At this point he thought it
best to continue walking without replying to the
last line and turned into niche of the petty
bourgeois.

Yes, he had indeed lived in the asylum, a
huge Victorian community of buildings neglected
and becoming derelict, as were most of the
patients, nurses and

doctors. It just induced that kind of nether world,
rich with the odour of brimstone. I opened the
wooden-side gate of the house because 'the
parents', preferred me to entered as surreptitiously
as possible, definitely not at the front door in view
of all the neighbours: 'there's the problem son,
they say the daughter is not quite right either',
Nobody will like it if I am an incarnation of a
flea…they get very worked-up about things like
that…mind you what doesn't freak them out.
'Hello mum, nice to see you'.
 'You didn't tell me you were calling, what have
you come for?'
 'Just came to see you as dad was at work so we
could listen to The Emperor, the piano concerto,
you know the Beethoven.' 'You can stop talking to
me in that manner, I'm quite acquainted with all of
the Beethoven piano concertos.'
 'Well, it's up to you; you know you're not allowed
to listen to your music when he's here…'
(this place was not my home, never had been in
any genuine sense, home was the itinerant life of

floors and sofas, travelling with few possessions, they were some scattered and treasured in bedsits, crash-pads…books. Always had one or two and paper and pen in the trusted shoulder – bag)

His mother replied: 'Well if it's cultural, you can come in and I'll make some sandwiches and we can listen; it's a wonderful piece of music you know.'

'Thank you mum.'

I recalled her telling me as a child that: 'When he played his piano concertos, he played them with such emotion that the pianos collapsed, were smashed.' We were both quite intense people; mum and I. What follows was certainly a dream experienced by 'the passenger' as a middle-aged man years after his parents' death.

What were the origins of his nightmare? Repressed unconscious desires, suppressed memories of occurrences to awful to recollect or his internalized fears cleverly manipulated by someone who had an agenda. Who knows where the origins of such an awful descent into such uncharted depths could be? The Narrator alone can stand without the lawyers brief or the biologist's microscope or the supposed privileged knowledge of the psycho-analyst. All she or he can do is to relate an experience. Here is 'the passengers' dream. He took his heavy night sedation as normal whilst listening to the news, within in an hour he was deep in a medication induced sleep, he'd been waking early for many years now, ridiculously early since his mother's death. As in many mornings now he woke around 4.00 or 5.00 a.m., he would apply himself to writing or studying; these were his main endeavours. Political and social isolation had lead to little other fruitful activity. On the few occasions on which he regained that allusive state, sleep, upon returning to bed he would fly through a most extraordinary galaxy of dreams or nightmares. Although disturbing, he was grateful for at least a little more physical rest because after many years he had become exhausted. Also they were of huge fascination to him, if not for others. That night he had woken around 5.00 a.m. but had felt pleasantly drowsy and soon returned to bed.

This is an account of what he then experienced whilst slumbering, wrote down immediately upon waking and passed this written record to me, the Narrator. This account is transcribed by me for the purposes of this short-story. 'He was travelling on the local bus out of town which passed a pub that was an old haunt of the revolutionary 'Left'. In those days he had lived a nomadic existence, sleeping on people's floors and took large amounts of amphetamine sulphate and L.S.D. but constantly read and wrote both poetry and prose. There were regular admissions into the local psychiatric hospital, and he neglected his appearance, but in a certain hippie style. On the bus he felt particularly alienated from the other people and estranged from reality. Upon reaching the village where his parents lived, he disembarked from the bus, he wasn't in a drug induced altered state of consciousness but felt separated from reality. When turning into the little street of detached, red-bricked houses where his parents lived, he was verbally abused by a group of young men, but made a verbal repost. As normal he knocked on the side door of the house because of his parent's position regarding the neighbours. His mother opened the door and eventually made him some sandwiches and they agreed to listen to their favourite composer, Beethoven. Mum sat on a three-person settee and he on the matching armchair. The black vinyl disc of an old EMI recording of Beethoven: 'Piano Concerto No 5 (The Emperor)' began to play, his father wouldn't allow the playing of classical music while he was in house. The 'familiar', a black cat of someone known to them appeared on the carpet. His mother began to shrink and metamorphosed into a hideous reptile, but as this occurred, she emitted a speck of dust which floated around the room. The cat began to swipe its paws towards the floating speck.

 His mother shouted: 'If the cat gets that speck I'm done for.'

The cat had caught the speck with its paws and was pulling it towards its whiskers, his mother was disappearing rapidly. As it was inhaling the speck he didn't know what to do, an atheist Marxist, he found this all very bizarre, but had previously considered the Roman Catholic priesthood. Not knowing how else to save his mother he dropped to his knees at the side of the sofa bent his head with his long hair in disarray and prayed to the Christian 'Holy Spirit'. The cat disappeared and his mother returned to her normal state. He asked his mother if she'd been watching Satanic video recordings of initiation ceremonies, she said this was true. He walked to the record player and removed the disc, splitting it into two as a Catholic priest would the Host at Mass; he then broke off a fragment in the same way a priest does before placing it into a chalice containing the wine.

 His mother took this and said: 'This will come in handy for our ceremonies.'

He woke and recorded an account in his poetry notebook, this is simply a transcription of the dream with no commentary by the Narrator or analysis by the dreamer, but as he recollected it upon regaining consciousness. As it is written. The passenger wondered, as the bus, the red bus swayed and muttered back to the dome, if on their grid the electricians made any brain cells that weren't fused: 'Cool that our 'scene' is not connected to their grid, hope the 'The Man' is about 'cause I'm waiting for him. Need 'gear' and a nice new set of 'works'. That was really heavy, know what I mean?

Book Review. 'On Dostoevsky.' – Susan Leigh Anderson.

Anderson's philosophical analysis of the ideas which motivated, or at least developed in, Dostoevsky novels is stimulating if not entirely convincing. Correctly she places Dostoevsky in the milieu of Kierkegaard and Nietzsche. However she then degenerates into an almost ritualistic denouncement of Dostoevsky's early revolutionary socialism for which he was taken to the point of execution and spent four years in a penal colony being deprived of books or writing materials. However the main thread of her thesis is based on ethics which she claims was also Dostoevsky's major interest and is indeed of importance. Dostoevsky's philosophical question was: How you can reconcile free will in the 'libertarian sense' with the concept of a God who is omniscient? The consequence is that God must have decided that evil in the world is a price worth paying for freedom. Anderson suggests that, for Dostoevsky, the solution was to create 'absolute values'. I, like Anderson, reject 'Ethical Relativism' but do not believe that the ethical values necessary to lead an 'good' life are enshrined in the heavens, indeed that seems a form of human alienation. The values necessary to lead an ethical life are rooted within Humanity itself, but these are distorted by oppression and exploitation and can only flourish in a socialist society. Dostoevsky describes his ideal world as:

'Universal communion of wo/men...the maintenance of complete liberty.'

These things can only be created by the proletariat sweeping away oppression and exploitation.

Breaking the chains: creativity and recovery.

'Many of the sincerest and most gifted artists and writers in this capitalist world are conscious of a loss of reality.'
- Ernst Fischer: 'The Necessity of Art'.
Some theorists of language, such as the 'Russian Formalists' have argued that this 'loss of reality' is a positive aspect to writing and the processes of language generally. The 'Formalists' existed before the revolution of October 1917 in Russia and thrived in the creativity of the post-revolutionary period of the 1920's, only to be crushed by the counter-revolutionary Stalinists during the 1930's. They moved attention away from the symbolist interpretation of literature to a more material approach to the text. What is of interest to us about them is the 'concept' of the 'defamiliarizing effect' or what they called 'making strange'.

The first step of their argument is that literature is condensed by Jan Murkowski:

'In the maximum of the foregrounding of the utterance, that is bring the act of expression to the foreground, into prominence for the reader.'

-

Murkowski.
The concept of foregrounding therefore is to put the 'linguistic medium' i.e. literature at the front of our perceptions. Victor Shklovsky argues this creates estrangement or a defamiliarization effect, by disrupting the everyday uses of language literature 'makes strange' the world of everyday life and renews the readers lost capacity for a new experience; essentially literature disrupts the

'mundane' which is part of our experience of alienation under capitalism. Therefore, it is possible to argue that a 'loss of reality' or even the process of 'making strange' can be understood as positive elements in writing. Having established the idiosyncratic nature of 'authentic' writing I will now construct a model of consciousness and language as formed by Marx and Engels which will then be developed by the philosophy of language created by Valentine Volosinov in the late 1920's. Then this model will be applied to the journey taken by Jean-Paul Sartre from his first novel of 1938: 'Nausea' which is a work of existential dread and horror which expresses the essence of Sartre's existentialism to his crowning philosophical text: 'Critique of Dialectical Reason' which offers a path to freedom through 'praxis' from the existential anguish of his early novel. Firstly then how did Marx and Engels conceptualize and therefore understand the categories of and the relationship between consciousness and language? The response is multi-dimensional to quote Terry Eagleton: 'Turned the whole history of philosophy of humanity on its head, revolutionized it with the statement:

'my method is movement upwards from the abstract to the concrete.'
- Eagleton.
This is the foundation for the overarching thesis I present here i.e. Historical and Dialectical Materialism. For Marx and Engels, we live in a material world. b) The material source of consciousness is material:

'Thought and consciousness are products of the human brain.'
- Engels.

This may seem obvious, but for many people the source of awareness is not the brain but 'The Idea' (Hegel), a 'First Cause' (Aristotle) or a 'Supreme Being' (Thomas Aquinas).

So, what is the nature of this 'consciousness' described by Engels?

'First came labour; after it, and then side by side with it, articulate speech.' - Engels.

This process is social and the result of people not only interacting with their environment but each other:

'in order to produce they enter into definite connections and relations with one another, and within these social connections and relations do their activity take place.'
- Marx.

Therefore, labour and language are social in nature. This position is developed further:

'First labour, then articulate speech was the two main stimuli under the influence of which the brain of the ape gradually changed into the human brain. The development of labour brought the members of the community more closely together...these relations gave rise to the need for primitive man to speak and communicate with each other.'
- Schneierson.

Here, therefore, is the fundamental model on which this thesis is constructed upon. Now I will look at two models of language in the light of the model constructed above. First, Ferdinand de

Saussure in his 'Course of General Linguistics'(1913) created a theory which would influence all following study of language. It consisted of: a) There exists a pre-established or ahistorical structure of language before its realization as writing and speech. b) It consisted of chains of 'signs'. Each 'sign' is made up of 1) Signifier which is the sound or written image of 2) the Signified or meaning/concept. e.g. in English the signifiers' T r e e is related to the signified Tree and therefore creates the word TREE. But this is random because in other languages the signified tree would have a different signifier... Because for Saussure this structure is detached from socio-history it is profoundly opposed to Marxism, but a Russian Marxist linguist named Valentine Voloshinov took it up in a study called 'Marxism and the Study of Language' (1929). He accepted the concept of the 'sign':

'The entire reality of a word is absorbed in being a 'sign'.
-- Voloshinov.
However, ideology which here means both ideas and 'false consciousness' (Marx) is transmitted through language:
'everything ideological possesses semiotic (sign) value'.
- ibid.
So for Voloshinov the false dichotomy between the material base and ideological superstructure of classical Marxism is resolved through language or 'signs'. However he recognizes the limitations of the 'sign' 'Signs only arise...they become material only socially, they comprise a group and only then do they take (real) shape.' -ibid. But it is when

'sign' or words become what Saussure had called 'parole' or 'utterances' that they become significant i.e. both material and socially interactive. Language is as Engels had argued a defining human characteristic. Voloshinov enhances this position:

'In point of fact, the word is a two-sided act. It is determined equally by whose word it is and for whom it is meant.'

The 'word' therefore introduces not monologue but dialogue...we communicate with others, he concludes:

'A word is the product of the reciprocal relationship between speaker and listener. Each and every word the 'one in relation to the other.' - ibid.

I would now like to apply this theoretical construct to the journey taken by Jean-Paul Sartre from the existentialist 'dread' of his novel 'Nausea'(1938) to the concept of 'praxis' as a path to freedom in 'Critique of Dialectical Reason'(1960). A path through human creativity as social rather than merely individual which can be seen as the solution to 'absurdity' characterized as mental health issues. The central character in 'Nausea' says.

'The nausea has not left me; I think it will be some time before it does...it is no longer an illness or a passing fit: it is I.'

- Sartre (1938).

The words nausea or sickness appear in two others of Sartre's works; 1) 'The Psychology of the Imagination' (1940) 'are conscious of a nauseating sickness.' and 2) in his first major philosophical work 'Being and Nothingness' (1943) 'dullness...feeling of sickness.' Why? Sartre defines three modes of being a) 'Being-in-itself' this are objects which simply exist like a tree, b) 'Being-for-itself' this is humanity, because we have no pre-determined essence, there is no 'First Cause', for Sartre, we make ourselves, we create ourselves. It is the absurd contrast between these two forms of being which is one cause for Nausea, c) 'Being-for-Others', here Sartre says we only become aware of our 'being' when in the 'gaze' of another, when someone 'looks' at you. Thus:

'I find myself in a state of instability in relation to the Other.'

- Sartre (1943).

This is where Sartre's infamous phrase

'Hell is other people'

Is derived from any belief in a system of ideas or faith was, according to Sartre at this time, 'bad faith'. But Sartre discovered the analytical tools provided by Marx and Engels and renewed them in order to explain and transcend this existential dread or 'Nausea' in 'Critique of Dialectical Reason': 1) he embraced Marx's concept of conscious human activity as the dynamic of History, once this was established he had to explain his early position of 'Nausea', 2) in order to achieve this Sartre created the idea of the 'Practico-inert' which is when humans are active but not social like atoms whirling around in a system and 3) he provided the solution of 'praxis' or 'depasssement' (going beyond the existing situation). This is a refinement of Marx's concept of 'species-being' which was, he said, the essence of humans i.e. to act interact with the world and each other. For Sartre 'praxis' and 'activity' are at the heart of the solution. This 'praxis' is genuine social activity created and made two-way by language: 'We set off from the immediate, that is to say the individual fulfilling him/herself to the totality of bonds with others...absolute concrete people.' - Sartre (1960). The social is creative and the creative is social, they are only divided in a social system which has what Marx called the 'division of labour' between mental and manual labour and ultimately between those who are compelled to sell 'social labour', which is their creativity, and to those who buy and profit from it.

But the only way to prevent the commoditization of art is to abolish commodity capitalism; one is dependent on the other. But maintaining an active dialogue between artists and writers is a key step in breaking the chains of mental ill health and aiding recovery.

The House of Ghosts.

He had recently regained his memory, the doctors had crammed him so full of tablets he'd burst. They had overmedicated, almost killed him. Noel was piecing together the jigsaw puzzle of those last 9 months. The chill of winter was still resonant in the winds, but the warmth of spring breezes crept in occasionally, it was a period of not one or the other. He had finally located Beech View House. It looked a rather large house and he wondered you got in, in seemed like a block of white-washed granite.

No bell, but a metallic box with a button labelled 'press'. There was no reply, he pressed and pressed again, it must have been almost 15 minutes. What have they done to mum, this place? A short, rotund man of about 40 opened the door:

'Hello, my name is Noel, Mrs Price's son.'

'Yes, well...' 'Um, do you think I could see my mum? Unfortunately, I haven't been able to visit because... ' 'Mrs Price's son. Oh yes I remember being told about you.' A wave of fear broke onto his wind-swept beach. The tides had always caused the sands to shift at the best of times.

'...I'm her son Noel. I've been in hospital, sorry.' He stammered.

'So we've gathered.' The care-worked retorted sharply, it strike like a jab with a foil.

'St. James', it's a ...' 'Loony bin.' Noel tried to be firm:

'A psychiatric hospital and I was in the general one, both. '

'I'm not here to talk about your problems!'

'Sorry I just wanted to see mum. We're very close.'

'Very close, what do you mean?'

'What I say conveys its meaning in- itself, I would have thought.' '

Don't you think you should be standing on your own feet, not bothering your elderly mother?'

'You misunderstand, I've come to visit her, have some real Turkish Delight from the bizarre, oh you know that specialist shop.'

'Bloody bizarre. Well come in, but we're about.'

There were people roaming along the corridors, some just bewildered, other muttering to themselves. They had lost what Sartre had called 'being-for-itself', nothingness drifting around in frail bodies. This place was indeed large, many houses knocked into one. He found Room 101, mum's room.

'Noel, thank God. You've come at last.'

'Mum, are you alright, what's been happening.'

'It is my younger sister; your aunt, she's had me put in here. Please take me away from this dreadful place.'

Noel gasped: 'You're not demented mum, I can tell. But I'm diagnosed with schizophrenia. I'm better with new medicine, but she's come down from up North, they don't know what's she's like. They will never believe us.'

'Son, it is a nightmare. She's ingratiated herself with the ingratiated herself with the doctor here. She went to the Court of Protection and had the Will changed, the doctor said I was incapable when I signed it.'

Noel thought quickly, the young aunt said there was a 'cool' doctor who was writing scripts for a gram of morphine a day. It all made sense now…

A 'fringe' performance of 'The Taming of The Shrew.'

 My performance is set in Victorian London. This is because Ibsen's play A Doll's House was reviewed by Eleanor Marx at that time. It takes place in a theatre with proscenium arch and curtain. The audience sits in darkness, the antithesis of Early Modern theatre. In front of the curtain is a table and chairs. Behind is the interior of a bourgeois house of 1880's. Petruchio dressed as Helmer swaggers from the right Katherina dressed as Nora sits on a chair. A ragged dress lies on the table: 'O mercy God. What masking stuff is here?' 4.3.87. Katherina is exhausted; she looks-up at her husband with fear. He holds the dress 'Why what a devil's name, tailor, call'st this?' 4.3.92 She backs away. The tailor enters from the left: 'You bid me make it orderly and well, According to the fashion of the time.' 4.3. 94-95. He smiles at Katherina:
'I never saw a better-fashioned gown.' 4.3.101. They smirk at the well-dressed man. The tailor says sarcastically: 'She says your worship wants to make a puppet of her.' 4.3.105. Katharina mimics the actions of a doll pulled by strings and she and the tailor laugh. Petruchio beside himself rages: 'O what monstrous arrogance!' 4.3.106. He staggers forward and tears the dress: Tailor laughs:
 'Your worship is deceived. The gown is made 'Just as my master had direction.'   4.3.114-115. The curtain rises to show Hortensio and Grumio who had been enjoying one of his cigars. Grumio and the tailor fight a mock battle, Petruchio and

Hortensio leave. The tailor and Grumio scamper into the wings on the left. The curtain falls leaving Katherina who lifts the hem of her

dress to reveal a small brown bottle of laudanum held in her garter, she smiles: From the wing the tailor: 'Why here is the note of fashion to testify,' 4.3.127. Eleanor Marx stands-up in the audience saying 'drama is the opium of the people' and reads these words:

'Women are the creatures of an organized tyranny of men, as the workers are the creatures of an organized tyranny of idlers'
        Eleanor Marx (1886) p.1.
 She ascends the stage and embraces Christopher Sly.
Marx, E (1886) *The Women's Question from a Socialist Point of View*, London,. Thompson, A (ed) (2003 2nd edn) *The New Cambridge Shakespeare; The Taming of the Shrew. Shrew, Cambridge, Cambridge University Press.*

The Cave.

The unexamined existence is all right for cattle, but not for human beings.'
- Socrates.

'Those who do not move do not notice their chains.'
- Rosa Luxemburg.

The winds whirled around the mountains and they chilled cruelly. It was another long day of captivity for those in the Cave, shackled to the ridges and hollows of the inner wall. These both cut into the flesh and it created the discomfort of bending to attempt to create some kind of ease for rest. A fire of wood undulating, almost pulsating with bright yellow flames and then heaving embers cast their shadows. They had been enslaved for a very long duration and, no one was quite sure amongst either the prisoners or guards for how long? The superintendent would only visit very occasionally but would always utter wise and high-flouting words, This did not ameliorate the circumstances of either the captives or their captors. Of course, all were stranded in a Cave halfway up a mountain and all they wanted was freedom. They had even forgotten how they came to be in this wretched Cave, but they were aware that the superintendent knew or at least that was the impression he gave with his protracted philosophical monologues. They could only be soliloquies not just because he was the superintendent but as no one else could understand, but one or two were beginning to get his general drift under the influence of a fellow prisoner. Something bout shadows and how these were illusions but that it what we saw we knew for certain. As we were chained face forward to the cave wall and the fire was behind it any man or woman could deduce, they were shadows. I can tell you the chains were real enough and the shackles and the gruel thick or thin that was our cuisine. For that matter those from the Elite Guard, handpicked to be our guards did not have a qualitatively different diet. In fact, we were all, if they could but understand, all the victims of the superintendent's obsession, his thought-experiment. However, I thought while we were stuck halfway up a mountain in a bloody Cave, bound by iron to the cave wall, great…the wonders of the Athenian State.

My discontent was beginning to be shared by some of the other slaves, not in the form of speech but by any number of hardly discernible acts of defiance; a bowl of gruel refused here, a refusal to stand there. Nothing that overtly the startled the guards because they were almost like somnambulists with the boredom of work and they thought in Formal Logic and we did in dialectics. Not what in thousands of years would be termed 'dialectical materialism' and 'historical materialism'. After all, would not Frederick Engels write in Anti-During.' The ancient Greek philosophers were all natural-born dialecticians and Aristotle, the most encyclopaedic intellect among them, had even already analysed the most essential forms of dialectical thought." Engels would develop this further, again in Anti-During, 'For dialectical philosophy nothing is final, absolute, sacred. It reveals the transitory character of everything and in everything: nothing can endure before it except the uninterrupted process of becoming and passing away, of endless ascendancy from the lower to the higher."   So now you see me as I am unfrocked, the scholar activist who lives and has always been present since those first hesitant incantations which would poetry and, later, prose. There will be tectonic shifts in the world called revolutions and then as noted by V. I. Lenin relations would one day be transformed: "antagonism and contradiction are utterly different. Under socialism antagonism disappears, but contradiction remains." (Critical Notes on Bukharin's Economics of the Transition Period)' Meanwhile back in our Cave the temperature was beginning to rise. What was this? Animal fat to ease the abrasion of our irons. So, some ethical considerations are being included as a variable in the great experiment. But the stench and now the guards are beginning to feel their status is being undermined by no one less than the superintendent, the philosopher Plato, pupil of Socrates of the subversion of the youth and the State enforced hemlock draft drunk to death. But what of this philosopher elite, or are we just but "cattle" to be cast in caves to proof some theory of Forms? Remember reader they used cattle trucks to take firstly, the psychiatric patients with black triangles. then the Left with Red Triangles, Gays and Lesbian with Pink Squares, the Roma and in 1941, and an attempt to eradicate European Jewry with a mocking gold Star of David sown into the anonymous black and white striped uniforms worn by all of those women and men, girls and boys transported around Europe to the industrial death camps. No, never reduce humans to cattle because you play with fire, that very elemental spark which makes us human. You can ascertain why the maxim of Socrates may not have been particularly welcomed in the Cave. After all we were little more than cattle in Plato's thought experiment, In fact his whole schema as delineated in The Republic placed the workers at the bottom, the military just above and those in flowing robes of white who were the philosophers at the pinnacle. The latter was very convenient and congenial for them. Why was I with men considered to resemble the bovine. It is rather straightforward because I too had been a pupil off a philosopher. I had attempted a little Socratic Discourse, but it was not approved off. A little too clever for my own good was the unspoken reaction. Don't let the pupil get any grandiose pretensions they sniggered. Although I pursued my course of asking rhetorical questions. Plato had said: 'Hemlock or you can help me in a little philosophising. I want to prove the validity of my ideas about universals, Forms, and you are just the kind of material I am looking for, a sort of participation philosopher on the spot. What do you say?' The bizarre thing is that it was presented as a choice, free will. I replied: 'I was always interested in the practical application of philosophy, …your philosophy, Master.' 'Good, that is settled then. The Elite Guard will escort you to the grand enterprise,'

He nodded to a few rather robust soldiers and that was how it had all begun. 4. But no, the animal fat was not to ease the open wounds which were encrusted with congealed blood caused by the now rusted shackles but to thicken the warden's gruel. This was like the moment a child realises the world is not a pleasant place and then I was confronted with the enigma. Was I to attempt to escape this imprisonment only to see the shadows were indeed caused by the fire or to foster discontent amongst the slaves in the cave? For I had already seen the other side of the fire, what lay beyond the Cave's gapping mouth and had nearly had to drink hemlock as my punishment for questioning the master philosophers. Should I attempt to negotiate some kind of truce between the elite philosophers and myself or did the resolution to this puzzle somehow lie in these men treated as cattle. The solution erupted into my head with the intensity of pure amphetamine taken intravenously. My mind was cold clear and crystal. The resolution lay in the slaves and soldiers realising their common social class which was not of the philosophers. A text written centuries later tumbled into my mind. George Orwell '1984', and the quotation from that misappropriated text that was strung across my lighting zig-zag consciousness was:

'If there is hope it lies with the proles.' But the proletariat were self-evidently only interested in whether their gruel was thick or thin or those in the cave. The soldiers although only marginally better off wallowed in the etch on the ruler of power and status and the philosophers had the banter to convince all was well in Athens. But different days would come Spartacus would rise and rise again resplendent. That could never, ever be quenched

I removed an eminently well concealed package of hemlock from under my testicles and slipped it into a particularly unappetising bowl of insipid gruel. There was no alternative in these circumstances but 'the living flame' will always contest the darkest night of History because 'the darker the night the brighter the star. 'My name, Walter, Walter Benjamin

Ward 20, a boy amongst men and Paraldehyde. (a story told from multiple points of view.)

Ernie, who was pleased to see me back on the light gang, pressed another yellow capsule into my hand. His face looked puckered like Charles Bukowski's, but Ernie was no poet. The capsule was a barbiturate called Nembutal; it would both wobble your mind but gave you a hazy buzz as well. Ernie, a man in his fifties had been prescribed these little beauties by ignorant quacks since his marriage. He had also been attending the hospital as a day patient to work on the garden's weekdays since that moment of matrimonial bliss which was immediately previous to the birth of a child. He never mentioned the child, only it's conception. I wanted to be 'clean' and had thought it would be safe now I was in a hospital. That was an illusion as you will discover. 'Thanks, Ernie I will drop it later.' 'There are more where that came from'. He smiled with the barbiturate saliva encrusted around his mouth. I mooched between the potting sheds and the Adolescent Unit until the coaches taking the day-patients, lurched away. There was a drain in near the Unit where I would unobtrusively drop these yellow submarines. However, Nembutal would be only one of my challenges and worries.

'Hello Noel.' 'Sister Leonard I was just on my way back to the Unit.' 'You had better hurry up or Auntie Edith will be chasing me out of a job and you back to 20's.' She said while simultaneously smiling. Auntie Edith was my name for the consultant, a true bluestocking. There was not much that Sister Leonard did not know about nursing under sixteens, apparently. For reasons that seemed unfathomable she had married a reptile of a man. The deputy-head gardener, John. He would evoke a combination of anger and embarrassment while he would tell intimate stories about himself and Sister Leonard in the potting shed. However, his repertoire was very limited. The urn chugged away on the hissing gas ring. Nine thirty and Fred as I am known, the gardener's assistant, had thrown in the tea, milk and sugar. It would be sure to be ready at eleven sharp and there were the cheese sandwiches to make yet. The heavy and light gangs were at work on the gardens. Victor, the head gardener was making cuttings in the glass house for the flowers which embellished some, well most, of the wards. The asylum I work in was like a clock whose cogs turned perfectly. That if they were wound correctly and not dropped down a drain. There was an excellent drainage system in this place. I have heard it called part monastery, part prison dependent on the state of mind of the voices. It was generally presumed by those living outside that it was an asylum. No, it was a psychiatric hospital. There are medicines handed out, syrups given, injections hammered home and electric shocks, not for those under fifteen though. But the rest, well yes. Let us not make bones about their ages? After all we would all be dust someday or so many have claimed I had heard somewhere. Sister Leonard mused as she measured out the tots of brown syrup Chlorpromazine, for her patients on the Adolescent Unit what a fine man her husband John and how wonderful that secret night of passion on a Cornish Beach had been.

Something that she and her soul partner would reminisce in quiet moments about all their lives. Whoops, mustn't be giving the kids too much Largactil as she gathered her thoughts. That was the medicine ready for lunch. Efficiency is the sign of a good ward sister she smiled. Again her thoughts wandered; such a shame about Noel, he was a nice lad but had got mixed up with the wrong crowd. The very words her mother had attempted to expunge her love of John with, parents!!

Joan was a handful, that is certainly correct I pondered. I shall bring disarray and chaos to this Unit. They say I am not ill. That stupid doctor had called me 'a spoilt little rich girl.' I don't understand why Noel will not be my boyfriend? I have done acid, speed, the lot. Could show him a better time than any of these nymphets on this Unit, what is it I puzzled. I will smuggle in some acid, that will do the trick. I will buy it on weekend leave. Why don't all the kids get weekend leave and why do a few, including Noel, get transferred to adult wards. Nobody transfers me anywhere except Mother and Father to this god forsaken place. 'To give you a little time to think about your behaviour.' At least I have some "behaviour ". There lives are so damned boring: no drugs, no kinks of any kind as far as I can gather. Yes, the Lysergic Acid arrived, and no one wanted to take it. Least of all me. She was not a nice person but stood a chance once she'd driven everyone else to distraction. That was why I did not sleep with her. She was a beauty but sometimes there is just a wrong thing to do. Indeed six months later on one of my early day passes to buy books at Hudson's in the city centre spotted me wearing a posh school uniform and cid create a leather briefcase. She glanced up, I looked away. It was for the best. The acid created mayhem, but no one was caught. Perhaps the nursing staff turned a blind eye...

Dear Auntie had sent me down to Ward 20 again. An adult but open ward. It was single sex like all the wards except for the Unit and Lambo Ward, mixed non-acute adult admission. Wards 19 & 5 being locked male and woman's admission wards, while 20s and 10s were the same accept but unlocked. I had got to know the staff quite well. Some would me books and we would debate matters philosophical, theological, psychological and literary. It was at this hospital that I was introduced to the ideas of Carl Jung and his Noble Prize Winner writer friend Herman Hesse. These later ideas were developed by a memorable senior registrar on the Unit, Helen. However, I am on my timed return visits both to the Unit and the Gardens when a very poorly man in his forties is brought in convinced he was a cook-coo. He is a lecturer from Birmingham University but has lost the plot to the extent that play was over. The staff ask me to find if he had taken Lysergic Acid, he had. I had never seen anything akin to this. He could se his feathers and kept jumping off tables, beds, wardrobes, anything and waving his arms. They interview injected him with Chlorpromazine, Haloperidol but nothing brought him down. Ward 20 was a bungalow and he tried to get onto the roof. This is three days and nights later, L.S.D. wears off after about eight hours. The door was so well unhinged no one could close it. The consultant arrives and leaves and the charge-nurse begun to draw up another injection into a glass syringe.

 'What are you giving him now. Why the glass syringe.' I ask. '

Noel, this would melt any plastic one.'

'What is it called.'

'Paraldehyde.'

Easter and beyond.

And what excess of love bewildered them till they
died?
I write it out in verse MacDonald and MacBride
And Connelly and Pearse Now and in time to be,
Whenever green is worn,
Are changed, changed utterly
A terrible beauty is born –
> -   W. B. Yeats *Easter 1916.*
>   [extract] (1988) pp 296-298.

You may wonder what I was doing in Finsbury
Park. We Catholics are indeed everywhere we are
ubiquitous. Here in England many think of us as
almost like dirty pests. Although we had always
observed their behaviour with interest and often
alarm. We always travelled light and took notes on
those who regarded us as parasites. This is my
tale, the tale of an everyday Mary. A woman who
had a variety of Holy statues in her flat: The
Sacred Heart of Jesus, Our Lady Immaculate and
lived with her teenage son. I am a trinity: a single
mother, my son and that echo in my mind which is
my father who had seen the inside of the H-
Blocks. A gust of cold wind whirled into my small
council flat in North London and I shivered as I
saw a faint spectral almost undefinable figure
hover briefly above my Holy statues. These
broken windows were becoming a problem; the
neighbours were gossiping; the social worker was
becoming suspicious and simply the price of
paying the glazier was becoming a task in itself. I
had many tribulations and the consensus woven
into the local fabric was that they mainly emanated

from Joseph, my son. People said it was a little more than the usual growing pains all teenagers are stung with when they stumble into that hornet's nest of metamorphosis called adolescence. I swept up the slivers of glass and called a glazier who I did business with yet again. There was no question of a call to the council for repairs as they had begun asking awkward questions. He replaced the window, puttied it in and said: 'I hope you don't mind me saying this, but it is costing you a fortune Mary. You must be pleased I did the job on the cheap.' I tried not to grimace lowering a veil of lace and then replied: 'And I hope you would not be concerned if I said that it helps keep you in business, Mr O'Connor. The reasons I ring you are purely one's of business not social work, you understand.' 'Alright, alright. I was only trying to help.' He huffed and puffed out and slammed the front door. I noted a swagger in his walk. Maybe he thought himself better or was he afraid of the supposedly unpredictable behaviour of those who lived in our area. Or he could be undercover? Fidgeting more than usual when my eyes noticed what the time was. I wondered where my son had got to and then as if by synchronicity he erupted into the room: 'Where have you been?' 'Hi yeah mum, I was only at the Mosque.' 'Now what is a Catholic boy doing in a Mosque? That is not to say I am against interfaith relations. That one has got a bit of a reputation now in Finsbury Park and with the Brits generally. I have heard they have been some quite extreme preachers there: 'They are not called preachers, but Imams. Mother.' 'Alright but be careful Joe. I don't want a convert on my hands as that would take some explaining.' We smiled at each other in a pact of reassurance; pacts lead to the signing of Treaties and we both knew a Treaty is not worth the paper or ink. I had been going to Mass on a more regular footing since the windows had been smashed and replaced so many times. What I could not ascertain ascertain was why they were being bricked. Some local people knew my father had been in "the 'army', the 'Provo's'" during the war in the North and had done time in 'The Maze'. That was why I had left, well sort of anyway. There is a grapevine you would only understand if you came from a Republican family. It spreads in two ways, both in the community and to the Brits. I knew it had been a mistake to attend that meeting to set up a steering committee for an event to mark the centenary. One hundred years since Easter 1916 and the blood sacrifice of Connolly, Pearse, MacBride and others. I had been taught to recite Padraig Pearse's last words at his execution before I could read and became lost in clouds condensed from memory and reverie which then rained words: "The fools, the fools! - They have left us our Fenian dead, and while Ireland holds these graves, Ireland unfree shall never be at peace." I had not noticed that Joe had buzzed backed into the front room where I had remained after he stomped off to his Another letter had said she was forced to have medication and that made me shudder more than any ghost could have done. Joe had departed from the house and a silence as dense as crystal filled the void. I repressed thoughts of his father. Though I was becoming concerned about Joseph's increasing interest in a politicized version of a very fundamentalist Islam. It was beginning to dominate him. I was opposed to this on two levels. Firstly, there was the question of Roman Catholicism and secondly, that of the potential for violence and wrongheaded violence at that. It seemed my father's activity had been justified. But to get involved with a group who may well have been originally a Frankenstein created by the West. It was heresy politically and they were really an apocalyptic cult. This was a qualitatively different situation to what had existed in Ireland, and I had to draw a line. The line was soon crossed! The police arrived, they knew me or at least of me and my background. Joe had been arrested and was being questioned about 'conspiring with others to prepare for an act of terrorism.' Although as the conversation developed, I ascertained he hadn't as yet been charged.

'Hail Mary, full of grace, pray for us sinners, now and at the hour of our death'. I said with a stony silence.

It had become a pre-recorded response of Irish Catholics in these situations. A forty-eight-hour order was extended by the Home Sectary to twenty-eight days. No one in the official or unofficial Republican movement would sully their hands with this one. I was told in the deep recesses of an anonymous pub: 'It would not be in the wider interests of building momentum in the rank and file towards an end game of Irish Emancipation.' 'So, my son who is the teenage grandchild of a man who had been subjected to the horrors of the H-Blocks was now expendable because he had an inconvenient ideology' 'There would be no legal assistance. The decision has been made by the Army Council who as you have always known Mary is the legitimate government of Ireland being the direct inheritors of the authority of Dáil Eiermann.' 'A question of bloody 'Ecco Homo'1 more like.' In the Vulgate Bible the Latin phrase: 'Ecco Homo' or 'Behold the human' is said by Pontius Pilate as he washes his hands in an attempt to free himself of guilt for the crucifixion of Jesus of Nazareth. It was a dark, very bleak and wet journey back to Finsbury Park. When I reached home, I arrived drenched by the cold rain and threw myself onto my bed without changing my sodden clothes.

Whether I developed a fever I shall never know. A third apparition came towards me. This time there was no mistaking the figure, it was Bobby Sands, the first hunger striker to die in 1981 a poet and an elected M.P. His life and poetry were familiar to me; he had the status of a secular saint in Republican circles and beyond. He said tenderly: 'Mary, do you understand now W. B. Yeats was correct when he wrote in his poem Easter 1916: "Too long a sacrifice/Can make a stone of the heart" I awoke in a fever and my clothes were soaked with sweat and I knew my life had been irrevocably changed. Fortunately, Joe was released without charge as the evidence would not have stood in court. It was flimsy and circumstantial. A few weeks later in the afternoon we received a surprise visit from Mr. O'Connor. To his astonishment I immediately welcomed him into our little concrete nest. He sat down and without hesitation begun:

'This may come as a quite a shock to you. I am your uncle, your father's brother. He was killed on 'active service' and that is all you need to know. It is the Veterans branch of Sinn Fenn that now preserves Ireland's cultural heritage since the Good Friday Agreement, you understand?'
'Yes, yes of course.'
'They have bought you, Joe and someone Joe has never met. A young woman you last saw as a new-born.'
Joe exclaimed: 'There was no abortion?!'
O'Connor continued: 'They have bought a cottage in the rural West for the three of you. You will never 'want for anything."
'Joe, it looks like you have a family after all.' I said.
'And perhaps we all have a future.' He replied
    Our 'future' in Ireland was almost an idyll until the banking crash and recession of 2008. But although our endowments and thus, our income dropped life was warm in our cottage. A warmth of family and of gradually being accepted into the far spread but close-knit local community. How different from our lives in Finsbury Park, I thought. But prosperity brings many blessings but poverty or at least a lack of a surplus bring other spirits calling. Joe had inherited the spirits of revolt and it was enflamed by when he began to read about the social problems we were having in the Republic, the lack of housing while millionaires dined on Venison, the water-rates had become a big issue as well and the continuing question of partition were often on his lips. They were not merely the concerns of the young though. with the Unionist vote now a minority in the North it began to look like a 'revolution in a ballot box' was a real

possibility. Sinn Fenn had done remarkably well in the election in the South, together with some far-Left groups. There was talk of a minority progressive Left government in the Dáil.

Yet there was something else very profound that nagged at Joe. To be sure it was rebel blood. I knew it and as he grew-up so did he. Rebellion was in our blood. Not something to be treated with leeches or sedatives. My country was built on the tombs of Republicans and socialists like James Connolly. Because ours was a land not only of bogs and mists, it was fertile with the blood of the men and women who had created it, died for it and been murdered for their courage. The Eucharistic sacrifice. Joe was now a young man, no longer a teenager, and I had taken to wearing shawls and headscarves. I knitted thick (mock) Gaelic jumpers for sale to gullible tourists, mostly Americans but also a growing number of Brits. When would Joe find a girl, I wondered in my heart? Or a male partner for ours is a country transformed after the disgrace of the Church. Ireland had chosen an openly Gay Taoiseach in 2017, but he was no revolutionary, let me be clear. However, Sinn Fenn argued for Gay and Lesbian Rights in this humming new Ireland. Still, my heart and head were bothered.

Joe had been away at a Gaelic Football competition with some of the local young men. The knock on the door which every Irish woman of my generation fears came about 1.00 a.m. However, they spoke not with British accents but were Garda officers both uniformed and plain-clothes. Joe had been caught running arms to the North for the Continuity or as it is known the Real

I.R.A. I knew it was the truth this time. Joe was just like my father and had rebel blood coursing through his veins.

I wept, I know not why as I mused, maybe he was the incarnation of the 'model' Irish child that was never conceived by W. B. Yeats and Maud Gonne. If you came from my land and background your heart would also almost burst with pride. That is something you will never understand unless you had come from an oppressed people. So, I prepared for the years of prison visits that lay ahead, or maybe not I smiled inwardly?

Petra, daughter of the revolution and her life after release from Stammheim Prison (A tale about the S.P.K).

The dark allurement of revolution and sweet aroma of introspection are intertwining like phantoms in this squat in 1975. Petra, a small round woman of 19 is sitting in the smog of contemplation. Her hair is brown, untidy and short, it sits on her head like the crown of a recently resurrected Rosa Luxemburg. A brown tee-shirt with embroidered flowers around the neck emphases her plump physic and faded tight black jeans combine to say that she is a goddess of the underground and nymph of primordial night. Smiling vaguely at a middle-aged man who looks like he comes out of some 19th century Russian novel, perhaps he keeps a chronicle of the demise of his shrink into madness, she suppresses a smile: 'Comrade…but let's just cut the shit baby, what kind of crap are you lying down'. Peter slowly strokes a long ginger beard which seems temporarily, to Petra, to be creeping across the roach littered floorboards like a startled lizard. He mumbles: 'It's like the movement needs a push to tip the balance, the proletariat are in the mood for poetry, we have to become their calligraphers, you dig'. She sighs: 'O I dig man, I really dig, know what I mean' The rapid rattle of a typewriter sends waves of disturbance through their awareness, it's like an automatic rifle firing into a black chasm of zero, like the relentless march of the masses into nirvana, muses Petra. In her mind there are images like water forming into vapour, into clouds which sometimes obscure the sun, now they spill their seed upon soil in a shower or in a deluge, either to fertilize seed or to wash it away in a torrent. Peter is pondering whether he should scatter a little fertilizer in this garden, the Garden of Love, where iconoclasts are welcome and encouraged to participate in its rites. But he decides, with a jolt from the intellect, that everything is subordinated to the struggle. He wonders what the dynamic of the armed struggle is, some of its shadows were illuminated and a solution had surfaced during those group therapy sessions with the professor, now imprisoned himself for activities against the State and Capital, where they had discussed the dialectics of liberation. They had discovered that for them, those especially damaged by capitalism, that their situation was more complex than for their comrades without psychiatric problems, their liberation from illness was directly linked to active participation in the emancipation of all the oppressed, it must be an attempt to grasp the full implications of the "death of God", but more than that, it was to be an active assassination of God, of the patriarch and of all his oppressive relationships and the, consequent, rebirth of the child.

He murmurs to Petra: 'The struggle, all of it, is about regaining innocence lost when we were children.'

A shadow passes across Petra's face: 'Yea man, you're talking 'bout the armed struggle, call it just cool baby, self-realization, just getting rid of all the shit they put in the head.' Peter says: '"Have you read the poetry of Sylvia Plath?' 'Of course, 'Daddy'…that's hot poetry, it's really groovy."

'Sylvia had grasped something of the essence when she wrote that line: "Daddy I had to kill you"'. Petra becomes animated; a crimson flush was rising in her face: 'She wrote those lines, there're like furrows in my mind, yea know, "Daddy, daddy, you bastard, I'm through" that's just real man, wow, so real. I've something to tell you, I'm Lady Lazarus, yea know, like in the poem'. Peter's gaze tightens; he looks intently at this young woman: 'You attempted suicide?' 'Yea, I guess I did'. 'Do you have a name comrade?' 'They call me Petra.' The incessant bashing on the typewriter continues without relief, it is thumping through the wall and invading Petra and Peter's consciousness. This is the remorseless beating of History: 'I have a name, it is Peter. Take my hand daughter, daughter of the revolution' A loud explosion, a blaze of orange light flashes into the room, black smoke billows and then their disembodied screams re reverberate in the chaos: 'Shit, man this is heavy!!' Hard and sharpened steel voices jab them like poisoned spear heads: 'Freeze it's the police... don't move, down, get down you scum' Petra and Peter are thrown against the floor, then heaved up and pinned to the wall: Peter shouts: 'Resist them.'
Petra yells: 'Defy them baby, I love you.'

But Peter loved only one thing and that was the 'armed struggle.' He clenched his teeth until a carefully, indeed, medically concealed, cyanide capsule ruptured. Petra was stripped naked on the floor of a West German police wagon., sirens wailing, red lights flashing with a plastic gag rammed securely into her mouth but although Petra looked Eastward and had believed what

Ulrike Meinhof had said about 'actual existing socialism' in the East.' She had not been fully trained, either behind the Iron Curtain or the Middle East. Like the majority of the Red Army Faction/ Socialist Patients Collective members who did not die during commando activities or meet in a similar fate in Stammheim Prison they threw the book at Petra. Decades in the purpose-built prison until release as a State Pardon. As Astrid Proll, a comrade, has said: 'What exactly do they expect them to do?' Petra threw herself into work helping refugees in Germany, now Unified. But as W. B. Yeats noted 'too long a struggle makes a heart of stone.' Petra was 'star crossed', she did not stand a chance. She used a new generation of contacts and blew herself up outside a police station. Although, you may not be surprised that she left a document explaining that this was her nemesis for Peter's death. Petra never knew nor was told about the cyanide capsule that he haemorrhaged to take his own life. As D.H. Lawrence said: 'never trust the artist, trust the tale.'

The Swallow

The leaves began to brood into autumnal red,
crisp crimson just before the frost bites when she,
a swallow, fluttered in through an open window
they had forgotten to close. You could now peer
into another nest of nails. She noticed there was a
shattered pane in a smaller room. However the
main room seemed perfectly ordered, a black
leather three piece suit, a proud wooden cabinet
which contained a colour television, a dark brown
wall to wall carpet, a door ajar gave a glimpse of a
dark tan dining table. There were not the vying
aromas of the poor, the really poor part of this city:
in a word, it was 'bourgeois'. Or like a Ford factory
canteen replicated in every Ford factory across
the world. 1972 and The Blitzkrieg Man seemed
an unhappy man she noted. Why? Of course, his
world was like a ball on fire, a conflagration from
Saigon to Chicago from Grosvenor Square to
Stuttgart. There was the Viet-Ming, the Black
Panthers, that Tariq Ali and the Baader-Meinhof
Gang or as some would say, 'Red Army Faction'.
He believed it to be victimization, a digression of
Eve, of Pandora, she guessed.   There was no
shelter for him as he could not do as Jagger
spewed out while gyrating like a little demon
seeking oblivion in Gimme Shelter three years
earlier she heard: "Gimme shelter come on give
me shelter, it's just a fix away, it's just a hit away."
Immediately the swallow realized he was as
straight as a rod of iron and as stiff as the ruler he
measured everyone and everything by. She saw
swooping about that he seeks that inflated
reflection of himself in the looking-glass which

reflects his bourgeois wife as Virginia Woolf had explained in that little book which promised so much. Those pages lay open in her mind now. Like all who fly she knew that mirrors break and should not be stared at and spotted a crumpled invitation to that curved psychedelic groove which is etched in the mind by Lysergic Acid hiding in the corner. Yes 'acid', a method of psychological exploration, for some it burnt through the mind like a hot knife through butter, leaving it melted, a splodge. Timothy Leary hadn't anticipated that.

Eva lay flat out on the floor blooded, she observed, but absorbed blood like a sponge soaks-up spilt red wine. Eva staggered and seemed to her inspired with the primordial fertility of the first monthly curse, the first towel-less, pad-less, tampon-less bleed remembered by every woman, each generation. She straightened herself and spat out these words between her swollen lower and throbbing upper lips: 'Go on, why don't you hit me again just to make yourself feel like a real man?' Blitzkrieg Man's flash of lightning had hit a lightning conductor; he was earthed by the audacity of his wife the swallow imagined he thought that as a gentleman, he wouldn't hit a woman. Not the fairer sex who must be put on a pedestal and admired, that is for men like Blitzkrieg Man until they stepped down from the pedestal and became human... impossible, for him to knock a woman off her pedestal. He seemed to her capable of deafening self-delusion as most people expected the sun to raise and set: 'But my dear you have cut your lip again, do take more care... Here, take this handkerchief. 'said The Blitzkrieg Man. 'Just another male chauvinist pig, you just oink bloody oink, you honky motherfucker'. Brigitte, his ex-student daughter, yelled.

'Not all that again young lady. You are a pathological liar. I am a doctor so I do know the symptoms of nervous disorders, maladies of the mind, I will say it "psychiatric illness". Now the inside of an admission unit can become quite, what should I say, busy, you wouldn't like that, now would you.' The swallow watched as she grabbed her Little Red Book, a whirlwind unleashing: 'Mao says: "Political power comes out of the barrel of a gun."' 'You will respect your mother and father as well as your country I say, I insist.' He said like a robot that saw cold steel and salivated iron fillings. Fluttering she observed him writing on the wax tableau of his mind... what would happen if everyone did what Jagger and Leary advocated. There had been a growing amount of research into this so-called, what a pretension, 'counterculture', the Nation would grind to a halt. Of course, there was one Nation, just one happy family, not everyone could lunge around dreaming like drop outs. NO! All must work and boost G.N.P; (there he stood a gross national product she thought). After all someone had said, he pencilled a murmur of a memory, 'Arbeit macht frei'. He mouthed the words in carefully pronounced and refined English 'work makes you free'. Yes of course and what else could it do, Ford proved at their Dagenham Plant, symmetry is aesthetic perfection when it comes to the factories. She noted   his nib slipped 'cemeteries'. Eva had cleaned her mouth, applied the usual cosmetic necessaries, an abused bourgeois

woman would use the term 'necessaries' the
swallow knew and walked back into the living
room, 'a death chamber' she sighed. This was the
death of love and death of the family. Just one
veiled glance towards Brigitte that hoped for a new
dawn with her daughter's generation. That
masked smile told the swallow this talk of
revolution was a little extreme, but so was the
clenched fist in the mouth from someone who
cannot recall what he has done: 'She's young and
an idealist, you shouldn't be so hard on her.'
enjoined Eva. 'Me, hard on anyone, ironic isn't it. I
go out to work, support you all and have a
daughter claiming I have a resemblance to a piece
of pork.' These decomposing nests were sub-
atomic particles of the atom that was suburbia, the
atom had split and its flames and hurricanes
consumed Nagasaki and Hiroshima. The words
had already been fashioned into a semi-circle of
wrought iron 'Arbeit macht frei' above the entrance
of Auschwitz. Then the swallow remembered her
mother, a 'mental-defective', with the black
triangle sown onto her blue and white striped
uniform, herded into Auschwitz from the cattle-
tracks with the Jewish
people, the communists and homosexuals. That
was when she had escaped the womb and
became a swallow. She dived down and spotted a
copy of Hermann Hesse Steppenwolf opened at
the page which described a door with the sign:
'For madmen only'. She, the swallow, had read
Freud and embroiders this text which is sown into
your mind with invisible thread: "Dreams are the
royal road to the unconscious." Had Brigitte
passed through Hesse's door in a dream? She

saw a dark shadow haunted The Blitzkrieg Man. What had it all meant, those had been idle threats towards Brigitte about mental hospitals, and he was only trying to control her as he attempted to restrain a world which was hurtling towards a nemesis for the privileged, its coming is certain but its fruition not, she mused. She swept toward the end of her song and told that Brigitte was ill in the terms employed by psychiatry, but not by 'anti-psychiatry'. Brigitte had read how the S.P.K argued 'turn illness into a weapon' and that it was a sick society that had caused her malady, her 'illness.' An illusion the swallow had conjured was the story took place in England, yes that is correct, however, in West Germany Brigitte's Double was a member of Sozalistischespatentkolletiv (SPK). Brigitte transmogrified in 1972 from become one of the butterflies in the second generation 'Red Army Faction'. Brigitte's German mother had been a swallow. This swallow watched Brigitte pondering Shakespeare: 'I acknowledge this thing of darkness mine.' Brigitte didn't mess around, muttered Mao: 'we must draw a clear dividing line between ourselves and the enemy.' She whispered:
'Daddy, I have a little something for you.'
'Yes.'
 'I'm going to light your fire baby.'
 She smiled.   Brigitte then coolly sprayed his bedroom with bullets from her Sten Automatic Pistol and precisely riddled her father with bullets again and again to make him perform a little dance; the bullets jerked his body like stings make a marionette jump. Was it History that had pulled those strings? She produced a Luger pistol

placed its cold black barrel on her lap and waited for the 'pigs', the police. Her mother sat silent and stolid. The Sirens wailed, but only lure more into dreams of love which linger behind every bloody sunset. This swallow flew from this chamber knowing that she, those who read Daddy escaped having their hearts pierced by spears of fire as Sylvia's had been. She always had to fly high, higher, circling just to escape that icy stare and glare of Room 101.

Notes on 'The Swallow'

Terrorism' is often mentioned in the news but; my narrative is of another milieu, different 'backstory' and ideology. Plath (1985) Daddy remained central throughout the editing. The 'swallow' originated in Frame (2008) where Grace Cleave is transmogrified into 'a migratory bird' because of feelings of dissociation. She is a 'personification' of Existentialist freedom. Research included: Meinhof (1971), Cooper (1972) and S.P.K. (1972). I attempt to answer Dostoevsky (1864) whose 'Underground Man' was a reply to Chernyshevsky (1863) who created the literary 'New Woman' incarnate in Vera Pavlovna, there is an allusion to Chekhov (1896) in my title. The narrator is the 'swallow'; she's a limited omniscient narrator. This allows the reader to see the world through her eyes and allows her insights into the story, retaining some of the intimacy of the first-person narrator as well as the advantages of a partial omniscience; 'confessional intimacy' with some 'authorial distance'. I tried to employ 'dialogue' for both 'characterization' and changing the 'pace' of my story. There is some 'telling' as befits an instrumentalist story, the conclusion gains momentum by 'showing'. The "crumpled invitation" is an attempt to apply the concept of 'Chekhov's Gun' to 'foreground' Brigitte's madness which also references Dostoevsky The Double (1846). Throughout the story I use contradiction and paradox as a strategy to propel the reader's interest and 'defamiliarize' their experience as in dialectical opposed belief systems of Patriarchal Capitalism and a tendency within Western

Maoism. I utilize both simile and metaphor in my prose. My intention regarding the resolution of my story is to realize a combination of a 'Chekhovian Ending' with 'Instrumentalism'. Although the genre is Historical Fiction it is subverted by being narrated by 'the swallow' who must question the nature of Realism for she is a non-human narrator. It has a resemblance to the parabolic. The intention was to comment on Patriarchal Capitalism:

"Representation of the world, like the world itself, is the work of men;
they describe it from their own point of view, which they confuse with absolute truth." De Beauvoir (1972) p. 161.
Both Sartre and Simone de Beauvoir were Maoist sympathisers.

References.

Bennett, T (1979) Marxism and Formalism, Methuen & Co Ltd: London.

Chekhov, A (1998) [1896]) Five Plays: Ivanov, The Seagull, Uncle Vanya, Three Sisters, and The Cherry Orchard, Oxford: Oxford World's Classics.

Chernyshevsky, N (1989 [1863]) What Is to be Done? Cornell University Press: Ithaca and London.

Cooper, D (1972) The Death of The Family, Harmondsworth: Penguin Books.

De Beauvoir, S (1972) The Second Sex, trains. H. M. Parshley, New York: Vintage. Dostoevsky, F (1985 [1864, 1846]) Notes from Underground, The Double, Harmondsworth: Penguin Classics.

Frame, J (2008) Towards another Summer, Virago: London.

Meinhof, U {Red Army Faction} (2009 [1971]) The Urban Guerrilla Concept, Montreal: Kersplebedeb Publishing.

Neale, D. (ed.) (2009) A Creative Writing Handbook, Milton Keynes/London: A & C Black in association with The Open University.

Plath, S (1985) Selected Poems, London: Faber & Faber.

Shakespeare (1998) The Tempest, ed Orgel, S. Oxford: Oxford World's Classics.

Sozalistischespatentkolletiv (1984 [1972]) SPK: Turn Illness into a Weapon, Dresden: Trikont.

Electra Unbound: A Modern Tragicomedy.

The action takes place over 24 hours. Characters with some minor notes on direction.

Bridget. A young student dropout, she has aligned herself with the radical currents in Western anti-psychiatry and armed urban Maoism. These occurred in Western Europe during the late 1960's until the late 1970s. She is in custody after killing her father.

Dr. Winston Smith. A middle-aged male forensic psychiatrist with a particular interest in Jungian psychology and social science.

Police Superintendent Julia Mosley. A strict disciplinarian
.

The Swallow. [Off stage and illuminated by a spotlight when speaking.]

She sees all the dramatic action and comments upon it as she swoops in and out. A solitary and atomised Aristotelian Chorus who creates a Brechtian 'alienation effect.'

Eva. Bridget's mother, traumatized by her daughter's parricide.

Psychiatric nurses and Police offices.

Locations: A police station. A secure psychiatric ward [on a split stage].
A presidium arch stage.

ACT 1.

Scene 1 A police station, which in not like an ordinary one, but more like 'Paddington Green' which is a British high-security station and holding unit for politically motivated offenders. The officers have no visible 'ID' numbers BRIDGET is roughly bundled onto the stage. USR. Bridget: Get your filthy pig hands off me Uniformed police #1: Wouldn't want to touch that scum, she, it, killed her father. Shot the poor bleeder in his bed. What's your name? Are you really human or just a monster that looks like one. Look like a human, you'd have to put a bag over your head for me to fuck it. (pause) Officer #2: Come on we have to charge you. I am sorry about the language Bridget: I will only give my status which is 'international revolutionary' and a brief statement.' I am a sister of the international struggle between the forces of reaction and those of progressive people's liberation movements.' (pause). Bridget: I am human only too human. He was the enemy, my father, like it was personified, you know what I mean... He was oppression incarnate. Officer #2: Another wordy one. Officer #1: Educated cow. I thought you people were the toiling masses rising up. You seem like a bunch of spoilt kids to me. Bridget [coldly]: Don't call me 'a spoilt kid'.... I am a revolutionary woman, and I believe like Mao in 'Drawing a clear line between the enemy and ourselves' There is a struggle during which BRIDGET is wrestled to the floor, face down and her hands handcuffed behind her back. Chairs and tables are overturned Bridget:

You can kill me, but you can't kill an ideal, the movement. THE SWALLOW through a loudhailer Off Stage: The pigs think we are scum, but just look and learn. Draw your own conclusions and don't be deceived, I say again, look and learn.

EVA is USL in the psychiatric ward and two nurses are trying to give her sedatives; she is distressed and walking on the spot. They do not speak except to say: Nurse #2: Come on take the medicine you know it's good for you. Nurse #1: Now you don't want an injection, do you, so take the pills. Eva: My child…

Scene 2

USL BRIDGET from USR on her feet, but remaining handcuffed. Lunges towards her mother: Bridget You have betrayed woman, you made her dependent on 'the Other', the male, the husband, my father. Where is your 'sisterhood', any solidarity? between women? Shit, mother, don't you have a mind of your own. I guess that's a fairly vacuous question in itself. INSPECTOR JULIA MOSLEY enters CSR [possibly wearing the uniform of the 1930's Mosleyite 'British Union of Fascists' known as the 'Black Shirts'.] Mosley: The woman is ill; the young bitch is a criminal. Keep them apart and while you are at it rough that little whore up a bit. The police officer #1 hits Bridget with increasing velocity and rapidity, he is warming to his task. Bridget: AR, Arrr ah, you filth… not every woman is cruising for a bruising, you are…bloody hell that hurt…the dead. THE SWALLOW stands-up OFF STAGE and is suddenly illuminated by a bright spotlight. She holds a white placard, which has emboldened upon in bold letters: FASCIST PIGS. DR. WINSTON SMITH enters DSL and glides into the melee. He put the upturned furniture back in place and places the papers in their files: Dr. Winston Smith: The young woman seems irrational yet not in a delirium, I want to look into this a little deeper. Let me spend some time with her.

He then orders that handcuffs be taken off and escorts Bridget to the far edge of the USL.

Scene 3.

A secure psychiatric ward is eerily quiet as the patients are so heavily sedated that they forget when they are holding cigarettes. The cigarettes smoulder into fingers and then fall onto fire-resistant carpets. Dr. Winston Smith and Bridget are sitting in the seclusion of his office. On his desk is Jung, The Theory of Psychoanalysis and Leach's book about Levi-Strauss published in 1970 [with heavy underlining. USL Dr. Winston Smith: Now, I am going to give you a chance as I can see you are an educated woman. I have been reading some Carl Jung about his discovery of the 'Electra Complex'. He picks up the book which is heavily underlined: Bridget: I scribble all over my books as well. Dr. Winston Smith: Leach argues in a recent study that the message of Greek mythology is simple enough: 'if society is to go on, daughters must be disloyal to their parents and sons must destroy [replace] their fathers'. (pause) Yes, well he first mentioned it in 1913, just at the time he was breaking with Freud. Bridget: Is that a fact... Dr. Winston Smith: Do I note a trace of irony, of a lack of deference to the analyst. Bridget: Maybe. Dr. Winston Smith: So, may I ask what are your beliefs Bridget? Bridget: I think you have a fairly good idea doctor. Ulrike Meinhoff argues that in the urban conurbations in the West 'the armed struggle is the necessary prerequisite for the proletarian revolution.' I was a member of anti-psychiatry group at a university hospital unit, our doctors became convinced of the position that psychiatric illness was the product of the oppressive relations in society, particularly the family... taught us to become revolutionaries, urban guerrillas.' Dr. Winston Smith: And you killed your father... Bridget. He was an agent of social control.... he was a real brute doctor, he would hit my mother and then pretend he had no memory of it. Dr. Winston Smith: I see, oh dear I see. That is, I cannot see for I am blinded. I have no eyes, like Oedipus Rex. Bridget: You can 'see' if you want to.... you are part of the system of what Louis Althusser[8] calls the 'Repressive State Apparatus' as a forensic psychiatrist you openly control people and with 'Ideological State Apparatus' as a father in the nuclear family. I am making this apparent because ideology is insidious. It uses 'interpellation' or 'hails' people, they don't see it as 'false consciousness', but as their chosen beliefs, a way of life. The stage darkens and DR. WINSTON SMITH is bathed in red light Dr. Winston Smith:[with obvious physical unease] Steady on Bridget... (pause)

Bridget: Camus says there is only one serious philosophical question after realization; 'suicide or recovery.' Dr. Winston Smith: You too have read his Myth of Sisyphus? DR. WINSTON SMITH looks away and stares across the stage. The Swallow OFFSTAGE: A game of chess and the King has been placed in check by our Queen.

ACT 2. Scene 1.

CS. INSPSECTOR JULIA MOSLEY: Winston, why do you go easy on the young thug? She killed her father, which makes her a parricide. Should be hung as far as I am concerned. Dr. Winston Smith: She is a complex character, disassociated from reality. Or at least the reality of the majority of people. Inspector Julia Mosley: Do you remember, before they had us in Room 101 we were lovers, we met secretly. We thought our love was revolutionary. Dr. Winston Smith: It was, in a fashion, but it is easier to rebel against the morality of a system rather than the system itself. Inspector Julia Mosley: Easy and it was good Winston, wasn't it...? (pause)   Good and easy, ah... INSPECTOR JULIA MOSLEY moves her face towards him, he pulls away. No, I am sorry, not again Julia. Damn you. Swallow [off stage] Star-crossed lovers, no way man.

Scene 2. USL   In DR. WINSTON SMITH's office:

Dr. Winston Smith: Bridget, I am interested in your 'high-functionality', your ability to intellectualize all your problems, it is if you have retreated into that domain. Bridget: It is a rich land, but I can see where you are going. It has its benefits, but also…. well, I live there, you see. Dr. Winston Smith: I believe I do, or at least am beginning to understand. Now Bridget, you have helped me to understand the world, my role in it. Bridget, did your parent's show you emotional love, or were it all a matter of material tokens of a love that may or may not have been there. Bidget [sobbing] 'Love'… what is that… material security but love… they were, are, emotional cripples. Dr. Winston Smith [takes her hand]: I can guide you out of this illness. Bridget: What 'illness'.

Scene 3.USL.

BRIDGET paces around Dr. Winston Smith chanting incantations, he is not afraid: 'Eliminate all rational thought, Eliminate all rational thought, Eliminate all rational thought. So writes William Burroughs. (pause) Don't you see that in an insane world? to quote R. D. Laing 'It is mad to be normal''
Dr Winston Smith: Eureka Electra, I think I have got it.
 Bridget: Cool.
The Swallow [off stage] Solidarity, comrades and lovers.

ACT 3. Evening.

 Bridget and Eva are now on the secure ward USR. The nurses are hoping for a peaceful night… Scene 1. BRIDGET moves toward her mother:

Bridget: Mother, you must be strong. They will try and give you shiny white tablets or brown syrup. Don't take it, it is called Chlorpromazine will turn your mind into a rotting turnip and cause your limbs to jerk. Eva: Why would they do things like that to us, we are patients and the nurse says they only want to help. Bridget: Mother, they are cogs in a machine. They do what they are told. Eva: You really do understand how things are, my child. You are teaching with wisdom that astounds me. For the first time in my life I know what it is to be free. You have changed, beatitude, you remind me of St. Clare and all those 'Poor Clare's' living a life of poverty and serving the poor. The Swallow [offstage]   A mistake, very touching though. DR WINSTON SMITH ENTERS CSR. Dr. Winston Smith: Bridget, there is something urgent I need to tell you. Before they got to me I was a person like Winston Smith as in George Orwell's novel '1984'. I was a revolutionary of sorts, a utopian dreamer, but
they hammered me and I was re-socialized and became a forensic psychiatrist, I sold out, but I still believe 'if there is hope it lies in the proles.' Bridget: That is a quote from the novel. Dr. Winston Smith: Yes, of course I should have expected you to know.

Scene 2.

Bridget: Winston, my comrade. Today's conditions in the Western urban centres must be seen from an internationalist perspective. Vietnam is being

bombed, they are using napalm on children. Dr. Winston Smith: I have seen some of the photographs, it is awful, really terrible.
Bridget: Remember what I said about Ulrike Meinhof… (pulse) Dr. Winston Smith: No that is too much to expect.
Bridget: As Anglia Davis says: 'Revolution is a serious thing, the most serious thing about a revolutionary's life. When one commits oneself to the struggle, it must be for a lifetime.' Dr. Winston Smith: I am a doctor, I have a family. I couldn't leave them to fend for themselves. The Swallow offstage: That is a line that must be crossed both Ulrike Meinhof and Gudrun Ensslin did. Silence….

Scene 3.

Bridget: You will Winston. She embraces him and they kiss deeply. Bridget: That is how important the struggle is. Nurse #2: Bloody hell, they are snogging. The doctor and that woman, the one they brought from the police station earlier. Nurse #1: Little hussy. Nurse #2: What should we do? Nurse #1: They are both going down for a long time, I'm ringing the police. Inspector Julia enters CSR and produces a small pistol, not a service issue. Inspector Julia: You have betrayed me, everyone, everything. I will shoot you both dead. Bridget: We haven't betrayed love or the revolution. Winston freezes unable to move. Bridget grasps the pistol. Bridget: Unlike Desdemona I can pronounce the word 'whore' and you are the whore of the bourgeoisie. Take that. A single shot rings out.

Bridget and Winston run across the stage DSR and Bridget kicks open the door. They exit hand in hand.
A shower of red rose petals is thrown onto the empty stage DSL by THE SWALLOW and she sings The Internationale...

ON THE PLAY...

For Plato, art is 'shadow of shadows', Aristotle developed a systematic aesthetic: Tragedy is an imitation of an action that is admirable, complete and possesses magnitude... Virtually all tragedians... use these formal characteristics.... for in fact every drama alike has spectacle, character, plot, diction, song and reasoning. But the most important is structure of events. Heath (1996) p. 11. Aristotle wrote what has become a dictum for Western dramatists:
   Tragedy, then, is a representation of an action that is worth serious attention, complex in itself, and of amplitude; in language enriched by a variety of artistic devices appropriate to the several parts of the play; presented in the form of actions, not narration; by means of a pity and fear bringing about a purgation of these emotions.
                    -    Dorsch (1965) p. 38-39.

Electra Unbound: a Tragicomedy's main Aristotelian action is articulated as a dialectical process. Bridget is a revolutionary who transforms Dr. Winston Smith's Weltanschauung

while he in turn shows her the love she was denied as a child. It does, however, leave an unanswered question: is she in fact resolving her 'Electra Complex' or not? My drama is an attempt to employ Brechtian 'complex seeing' as defined by Raymond Williams in Aristotelian dramatology: ' It is not the good person against the bad, but goodness and badness as alternate expressions of a single being. This is complex seeing and it is deeply integrated with dramatic form.'
Williams (2006) p. 234-235.

This dialectic is enacted within the structure of Aristotelian Tragedy, but with a happy 'turn' at the conclusion transforming it into a tragicomedy. I try to make the play function on a cause-effect basis as Aristotle advised and use the 'dramatic arc' (Neale (2009) p 85). The main technical problem I encountered in transforming TMA01 'The Swallow' into TMA02 was that of how to incorporate the swallow who had been an omniscient third-person narrator into my drama. I attempted this by making her into an atomized Aristotelian chorus who was off stage, but with a presence, either heard or seen on stage and utilising the methodology of Brecht (2013) Life of Galileo where placards are used in Brecht's concept of 'epic theatre' (Brecht, 1964). I attempt to combine both mimesis and Brecht's 'Alienation-Effect'. The play begins with an allusion to Shelley (2009) Prometheus Unbound and ends with one to Ibsen (2008) A Doll's House. Bridget's chanting of Burroughs's in Act 2, Scene 3 is an attempt to make language chaotic and thus challenge its phallocentric nature

as achieved in the work of Hélène Cixous
'creature feminine' [feminine writing].

Bibliography

Althusser, L (2008 [1971]) Ideology and
Ideological State Apparatus. (Notes towards an
investigation), London: Verso.
Aristotle/Horace/Longinus (1965) Classical
Literary Criticism, trans, T. S. Dorsch,
Harmondsworth: Penguin Classics
Aristotle (1996), Poetics, trans, Malcolm Heath,
Harmondsworth: Penguin Classics.
Brecht, B (1964) Brecht on Theatre, trans, John
Willett, London: Methuen Drama. Brecht, B
(2006) Life of Galileo, trans, John Willett, London:
Bloomsbury.
Jung, C (1998) The Essential Carl Jung, London,
Fontana Books.
Ibsen, H (2008) Four Major Plays, Oxford: Oxford
World Classics.
Leach, E (1970) Claude Levi-Strauss. Revised ed.
New York: Viking Press.
Meinhof, U {Red Army Faction} (2009 [1971]) The
Urban Guerrilla Concept, Montreal: Kersplebedeb
Publishing. Mullen, B (1995)
Mad To Be Normal: conversations with R. D.
Laing, London: Free Association Books.

Lightning Source UK Ltd.
Milton Keynes UK
UKHW010651101022
410232UK00001B/228